Employers are responsible for providing a safe and healthful workplace for their employees. OSHA's role is to assure the safety and health of America's workers by setting and enforcing standards; providing training, outreach and education; establishing partnerships; and encouraging continual improvement in workplace safety and health.

This handbook provides a general overview of a particular topic related to OSHA standards. It does not alter or determine compliance responsibilities in OSHA standards or the *Occupational Safety and Health Act of 1970*. Because interpretations and enforcement policy may change over time, you should consult current OSHA administrative interpretations and decisions by the Occupational Safety and Health Review Commission and the Courts for additional guidance on OSHA compliance requirements.

This information is available to sensory impaired individuals upon request. Voice phone: (202) 693-1999; teletypewriter (TTY) number: (877) 889-5627.

Best Practices for Hospital-Based First Receivers

of Victims from Mass Casualty Incidents Involving the Release of Hazardous Substances

Occupational Safety and Health Administration
U.S. Department of Labor

OSHA 3249-08N
2005

OSHA
Occupational Safety and
Health Administration

LIST OF FIGURES AND TABLES

ACKNOWLEDGMENTS

OSHA's Directorate of Science, Technology and Medicine wishes to acknowledge the assistance provided by the following organizations: U.S. Department of Veterans Affairs (VA), California Emergency Medical Services Authority (EMSA), Centers for Disease Control and Prevention/Agency for Toxic Substances and Disease Registry (CDC/ATSDR), National Institute for Occupational Safety and Health (NIOSH), INOVA Health System, Northern Virginia Hospital Alliance, Kaiser Permanente, U.S. Coast Guard National Strike Force, and the U.S. Army Center for Health Promotion and Preventive Medicine (USACHPPM). OSHA's Directorate of Enforcement Programs (DEP), and the Directorate of Standards and Guidance (DSG), as well as the Office of the Solicitor, OSH Division (SOL) also made notable contributions.

Seven hospitals provided extensive information, hospital tours, equipment demonstrations, interviews, photographs, and reference material for this project:

Central Arkansas Veterans Healthcare System, Little Rock, Arkansas

Enloe Medical Center, Chico, California

National Naval Medical Center, Bethesda, Maryland

New York University Medical Center, New York City, New York

Samaritan Regional Health System, Ashland, Ohio

Sutter Amador Hospital, Jackson, California

Veterans Administration Medical Center, Washington, DC

These hospitals were identified by hospital organizations as having given notable consideration to the possibility of receiving contaminated victims from a mass casualty incident involving hazardous substance release. Hospitals interviewed were selected to represent a range of circumstances, loosely based on location (U.S. region) and the hospital's relative probability (risk) of receiving contaminated victims of a mass casualty incident. This risk was estimated using a scale adapted from the Hospital Corporation of America (HCA, undated):

- Key Treatment Centers – Hospitals in large urban areas. (Hospitals A, B, C, and G.)*
- Potential Risk Hospitals – Hospitals within 50 miles of a large urban area and high-visibility potential targets where a mass casualty incident could occur (e.g., major airport or sports stadium, large chemical manufacturing facility, nuclear power plant, major shopping mall, nationally recognized monument). (Hospitals D and E.)*
- Minimum Risk Hospitals – Hospitals with populations less than 500,000 within a 50-mile radius and without a high-visibility potential target within that distance. (Hospital F.)*

Note: This risk scale was used only to help identify a diverse group of hospitals for interviews. Other scales might have been used and OSHA does not promote this or any other scheme.

* To maintain a minimum level of confidentiality, hospitals were assigned letters according to risk category which do not reflect the alphabetical order in which they are listed above.

The following agencies and organizations reviewed and provided comments regarding these OSHA Best Practices:

Agency for Healthcare Research and Quality (AHRQ)

Agency for Toxic Substances and Disease Registry (ATSDR)

American College of Emergency Physicians (ACEP)

American Hospital Association/American Society for Healthcare Engineering (ASHE)

U.S. Navy Bureau of Medicine and Surgery (BUMED)

California Emergency Medical Services Authority (CA-EMSA)

Centers for Disease Control and Prevention (CDC)

Emergency Nurses Association (ENA)

EnMagine (hazmatforhealthcare.org)

George Washington University - Institute for Crisis, Disaster and Risk Management

Health Resources & Services Administration (HRSA), National Bioterrorism Hospital Preparedness Program

Hennepin County (MN) Medical Center, Emergency Medicine

Inova Health System, Emergency Management and Disaster Medicine; and Employee and Occupational Health Departments

International Chemical Workers Union Council of the United Food and Commercial Workers Union (ICWUC)

International Safety Equipment Association (ISEA)

Joint Commission on Accreditation of Healthcare Organizations (JCAHO)

Kaiser Permanente

National Incident Management System (NIMS) Integration Center

National Organization for Victim Assistance (NOVA)

Navy Environmental Health Center, Industrial Hygiene Directorate,

Navy Medicine Office of Homeland Security, Bureau of Medicine and Surgery

National Institute of Environmental Health Sciences (NIEHS), Worker Education and Training Program (WETP), National Clearinghouse for Worker Safety and Health Training

National Institute for Occupational Safety and Health (NIOSH)

NYU Medical Center, Environmental Services Department

Rhode Island Department of Health

Samaritan Regional Health System

University of Maryland School of Medicine, National Study Center for Trauma & EMS

U.S. Department of Veterans Affairs, Central Arkansas Veterans Healthcare System

U.S. Department of Veterans Affairs, Office of Occupational Safety and Health

U.S. Department of Veterans Affairs, Occupational Health Program

U.S. Department of Veterans Affairs, Veterans Administration Medical Center (Washington, DC)

U.S. Army Center for Health Promotion and Preventive Medicine (USACHPPM)

EXECUTIVE SUMMARY

Healthcare workers risk occupational exposures to chemical, biological, or radiological materials when a hospital receives contaminated patients, particularly during mass casualty incidents. These hospital employees, who may be termed first receivers, work at a site remote from the location where the hazardous substance release occurred.[1] This means that their exposures are limited to the substances transported to the hospital on victims' skin, hair, clothing, or personal effects (Horton et al., 2003). The location and limited source of the contaminant distinguishes first receivers from other first responders (e.g., firefighters, law enforcement, and ambulance service personnel), who typically respond to the incident site (i.e., the Release Zone).

In order to protect their employees, hospitals benefit from information to assist them in emergency planning for incidents involving hazardous substances (BNA, 2003; Barbera and Macintyre, 2003). Emergency first responders, at the site of the release, are covered under OSHA's standard on Hazardous Waste Operations and Emergency Response (HAZWOPER), or the parallel OSHA-approved State Plan standards, and depending on their roles, some hospital employees also are covered by the standard.[2,3] However, OSHA recognizes that first receivers have somewhat different training and personal protective equipment (PPE) needs than workers in the hazardous substance Release Zone, a point clarified through letters of interpretation (OSHA, 2002a).

In this best practices document, OSHA provides practical information to help hospitals address employee protection and training as part of emergency planning for mass casualty incidents involving hazardous substances. OSHA considers sound planning the first line of defense in all types of emergencies (including emergencies involving chemical, biological, or radiological substances). By tailoring emergency plans to reflect the reasonably predictable "worst-case" scenario under which first receivers might work, the hospital can rely on these plans to guide decisions regarding personnel training and PPE (OSHA, 2003, 2002b, 1999). The Joint Commission on Accreditation of Healthcare Organizations (JCAHO) requires an all-hazard approach to allow organizations to be flexible enough to respond to emergencies of all types, whether natural or manmade (unintentional or intentional).[4]

Worst-case scenarios take into account challenges associated with communication, resources, and victims. During mass casualty emergencies, hospitals can anticipate little or no warning before victims begin arriving.[5] Additionally, first receivers can anticipate that information regarding the hazardous agent(s) would not be available immediately. Hospitals also can anticipate a large number of self-referred victims (as many as 80 percent of the total number of victims) and assume victims will not have been decontaminated prior to arriving at the hospital (Auf der Heide, 2002; Barbera and Macintyre, 2003; Vogt, 2002; Okumura et al., 1996).

The appropriate employee training and PPE selection processes are defined in applicable OSHA standards.[6] An employee's role and the hazards that an employee might encounter dictate the level of training that must be provided to any individual first receiver.

---

[1] Hazardous substance is defined as any substance to which exposure may result in adverse effects on the health or safety of employees. This includes substances defined under Section 101(14) of CERCLA; biological or disease-causing agents that may reasonably be anticipated to cause death, disease, or other health problems; any substance listed by the U.S. Department of Transportation as hazardous material under 49 CFR 172.101 and appendices; and substances classified as hazardous waste.

[2] 29 CFR 1910.120.

[3] First responders, including firefighters, law enforcement, and emergency medical personnel, and many first receivers at public hospitals, are usually employees of local, municipal, or state governments. Although Federal OSHA's standards and enforcement authority do not extend to such state and local governments, these employers and employees are covered by the 26 states that operate OSHA-approved State Plans and, in states without State Plans, by the Environmental Protection Agency (EPA) with regard to HAZWOPER (29 CFR 1910.120). State Plan states set and enforce standards, such as the HAZWOPER and Respiratory Protection standards, which are identical to or "at least as effective as" Federal OSHA standards, and therefore may have more stringent or supplemental requirements. EPA's HAZWOPER parallel standard was adopted to cover emergency responders who would not be covered by the OSHA standard, including volunteers who work for a governmental agency engaged in emergency response, such as firefighters. For consistency, OSHA interprets the HAZWOPER Standard for the EPA. Federal OSHA administers the safety and health program for the private sector in the remaining states and territories, and also retains authority with regard to safety and health conditions for Federal employees throughout the nation (OSHA, 1991c).

[4] Note: Footnotes at relevant points in the text indicate current JCAHO Standards for Emergency Management, which are further described in Section EC 1.4 of JCAHO's Comprehensive Accreditation Manual (JCAHO, 2004).

[5] Mass casualty may be defined as "a combination of patient numbers and patient care requirements that challenges or exceeds a community's ability to provide adequate patient care using day-to-day operations" (Barbera and Macintyre, 2003).

[6] Applicable OSHA standards include: 29 CFR 1910.120 – HAZWOPER; 29 CFR 1910.132 – Personal Protective Equipment – General Requirements; 29 CFR 1910.133 – Eye and Face Protection; 29 CFR 1910.134 – Respiratory Protection.

PPE selection must be based on a hazard assessment that carefully considers both of these factors, along with the steps taken to minimize the extent of the employee's contact with hazardous substances.

Despite many hospitals' strong interest in powered air-purifying respirators (PAPRs) as a practical form of respiratory protection for first receivers in the Hospital Decontamination Zone, many knowledgeable sources avoid making specific PPE recommendations, but rather point out the advantages and disadvantages of the various options, or recommend *appropriate* PPE (JCAHO, 2001; Lehmann, 2002; Penn, 2002). Others offer stronger opinions. CA EMSA (2003a) promotes the use of a multi-tiered approach to PPE. Burgess (1999) indicates, in an article published prior to more recent letters of interpretation specific to healthcare workers, that OSHA requires Level B protection or self-contained breathing apparatus (SCBA) for unknown hazards, but points out that there are substantial difficulties for healthcare workers who attempt to care for patients while wearing this type of equipment and also addresses the hazards of wearing SCBAs (e.g., slips, trips, falls, and overexertion, particularly for infrequent users of this equipment). These sources demonstrate appropriate caution in the face of unknown contaminants of unknown concentration. However, OSHA believes that the substantial body of recent information on first receivers' actual experiences and probable exposure levels now allows more definitive guidance.

In this best practices document, OSHA specifies PPE that hospitals could use to effectively protect first receivers assisting victims contaminated with *unknown substances*, provided the hospital meets certain prerequisite conditions designed to minimize the quantity of substance to which first receivers might be exposed. This PPE for first receivers includes: a PAPR with an assigned protection factor of 1,000, a chemical-resistant protective garment, head covering if it is not already included in the respirator, a double layer of protective gloves, and chemical-protective boots (see Table 3 at page 23). As part of OSHA's required hazard assessment process, each hospital also must consider the specific hazards first receivers might reasonably be expected to encounter.[7] The hospital must then

augment OSHA's PPE selection when necessary to provide adequate protection against those specific identified hazards.

The specified PPE is appropriate when the hazardous substance is unknown and the concentration is strictly limited by (1) the quantity of material associated with living victims *and* (2) the conditions, policies, equipment, and procedures that are in place and that will reduce employee exposure. Tables 1 and 2 of the best practices document list those specific prerequisites that OSHA believes are necessary to adequately limit first receiver exposures and to assure the adequacy of the PPE presented in Table 3. Such conditions include a current Hazard Vulnerability Analysis (HVA) and emergency management plan (EMP), as well as procedures to ensure that contaminated materials are removed from the area and contained so they do not present a continuing source of exposure.

The first receiver PPE listed in Table 3 is not the only option for first receivers. Employees at hospitals that do not meet the criteria shown in Tables 1 and 2 must determine whether more protective equipment is required (e.g., HAZWOPER Level B). A higher level of protection also may be necessary for any hospital that anticipates providing specialized services (such as a Hazardous Materials Response Team at the incident site). Additionally, if a hospital is responding to a known hazard, the hospital must ensure that the selected PPE adequately protects the employees from the identified hazard. Thus, hospitals must augment or modify the PPE in Table 3 if the specified PPE is not sufficient to protect employees from the identified hazard. Alternatively, if a hazard assessment demonstrates that the specified PPE is not necessary to effectively protect workers from the identified hazard, a hospital would be justified in selecting less protective PPE, as long as the PPE actually selected by the hospital provides effective protection against the hazard.

This best practices document provides hospitals and other health care providers with information to assist in the provision of PPE and training for first receivers. The first section introduces the subject, while the second section provides a detailed analysis of potential hazards, as well as a comprehensive discussion of the PPE currently available to protect work-

---

[7] These specific hazards will be identified in the hospital's hazard vulnerability analysis (HVA). JCAHO Standards for Emergency Management require hospitals to: (1) develop a comprehensive emergency management plan (EMP) describing the hospital's response to emergencies that would affect the need for the hospital's services or the hospital's ability to provide these services; (2) evaluate the EMP annually including the objectives, scope, functionality, and effectiveness; (3) conduct an HVA, to identify potential emergences that could affect the need for the hospital's services, or its ability to provide these services; and (4) identify the hospital's role in the community and coordinate plans.

ers from these hazards. In the Personal Protective Equipment section OSHA provides three tables designed to assist employers in selecting PPE adequate to protect healthcare workers and to comply with relevant OSHA PPE standards. Employers who meet the prerequisites in Tables 1 and 2 may use this best practices document as the OSHA-required generalized hazard assessment. Such employers may choose to rely on the PPE specified in Table 3 to comply with relevant OSHA standards and to provide effective protection for first receivers against a wide range of hazardous substances. However, such employers also must conduct a hazard assessment that considers hazards unique to the community in which they are located. In rare situations, these employers will need to augment or modify the PPE specified in Table 3 to provide adequate protection against unique hazards identified in the community-specific hazard analysis. Of course, employers are not obligated to follow the guidance in Table 3; any employer can choose instead to perform an independent hazard assessment that is sufficient to identify the hazards that its employees are reasonably anticipated to encounter, and then select PPE adequate to protect its employees against such hazards. The Training First Receivers section of this best practices document contains a discussion of training required for first receivers and concludes with Table 4, which matches required training levels to employee roles and work areas.

Appendix A of this best practices document provides background information on how various aspects of a hospital's preparation, response, and recovery impact employee protection during hazardous substance emergencies. Appendices B, C, and D list additional information sources, while Appendices E through M offer examples of procedures and equipment used in some hospitals. OSHA offers these examples for informational purposes only and does not recommend one option over the many effective alternatives that exist. Emergency managers might find these resources helpful in developing or updating existing EMPs.

This document is based on presently available information as well as current occupational safety and health provisions and standards. Employers should modify their procedures as appropriate when additional, relevant information becomes available or when modifications to Occupational Safety and Health Act (OSH Act) or JCAHO standards necessitate revision. The OSH Act requires employers to comply with hazard-specific safety and health standards. In addition, pursuant to Section 5(a)(1), the General Duty Clause of the OSH Act, employers must provide their employees with a workplace free from recognized hazards likely to cause death or serious physical harm. This document incorporates existing applicable regulatory provisions as well as non-mandatory work practices and methods that may be implemented to further supplement employee protection against exposure to hazardous substances. OSHA has attempted to clearly distinguish between mandatory and recommended work practices/methods within this document. Where regulations establish performance criteria for compliance, this document attempts to provide specific guidance that employers may use to adequately protect employees and comply with these regulatory provisions. However, an alternative approach may be justified given specific workplace circumstances. This document does not enlarge or diminish an employer's obligations under the OSH Act.

BACKGROUND

Healthcare workers risk occupational exposure to chemical, biological, or radiological materials when hospitals receive patients contaminated with these substances during mass casualty incidents (Horton et al., 2003).[8] Such incidents could be associated with man-made (intentional or unintentional) or natural disasters and can involve a wide range of hazardous substances—from chemical weapons agents to toxic industrial chemicals (Horton et al., 2003).

DEFINING "FIRST RECEIVERS"

Healthcare workers at a hospital receiving contaminated victims for treatment may be termed *first receivers* (Koenig, 2003). This group is a subset of *first responders* (e.g., firefighters, law enforcement, HAZMAT teams, and ambulance service personnel). However, most first responders typically act at the site of an incident (i.e., the location at which the primary release occurred). In contrast, inherent to the definition of first receivers is an assumption that the hospital is not itself the primary incident site, but rather is remote from the location where the hazardous substance release occurred. Thus, the possible exposure of first receivers is limited to the quantity of substance arriving at the hospital as a contaminant on victims and their clothing or personal effects (Horton et al., 2003).

First receivers typically include personnel in the following roles: clinicians and other hospital staff who have a role in receiving and treating contaminated victims (e.g., triage, decontamination, medical treatment, and security) and those whose roles support these functions (e.g., set up and patient tracking).[9]

SCOPE AND OBJECTIVES

In order to protect their employees, hospitals benefit from information to assist them in emergency planning for incidents involving hazardous substances (BNA, 2003; Barbera and Macintyre, 2003). Emergency first responders at the scene of the incident, including fire, law enforcement, and emergency medical personnel, are covered by the requirements of OSHA's

standard on Hazardous Waste Operations and Emergency Response (HAZWOPER), or by parallel state standards in states with OSHA-approved State Plans.[10,11] However, the extent of the hazard to the hospital-based first receivers (a subgroup of first responders) can differ from that at the release site. A series of OSHA letters of interpretation clarifies when and how the HAZWOPER standard applies to first receivers. This best practices document provides information useful to employers attempting to provide adequate protection for hospital-based first receivers during mass casualty incidents involving hazardous substances.

Specifically, this best practices document covers protection for first receivers during releases of chemicals, radiological particles, and biological agents (overt releases) that produce victims who may need decontamination prior to administration of medical care. Although intended for mass casualty incidents as they affect emergency department personnel at fixed hospitals, the basic principles and concepts of this guidance also apply to mobile casualty care facilities and temporary shelters, such as would be necessary in the event of a catastrophic incident involving tens or hundreds of thousands of victims.

The scope of this best practices document does **not** include situations where the hospital (or temporary facility) is the site of the release. Nor does it include infectious outbreaks for which victim decontamination is **not** necessary.

---

[8] For the purposes of this guidance, OSHA uses the definition of *mass casualty* provided by Barbera and Macintyre (2003): "A combination of patient numbers and patient care requirements that challenges or exceeds a community's ability to provide adequate patient care using day-to-day operations."

[9] The term *clinician* refers to physicians, nurses, nurse practitioners, physicians' assistants, and others.

---

[10] HAZWOPER 29 CFR 1910.120.

[11] First responders, including firefighters, law enforcement and emergency medical personnel, and many first receivers at public hospitals, are usually employees of local, municipal or state governments. Although Federal OSHA's standards and enforcement authority do not extend to such state and local governments, these employers and employees are covered by the 26 states that operate OSHA-approved State Plans and, in states without State Plans, by the Environmental Protection Agency (EPA) with regard to HAZWOPER (29 CFR 1910.120). State Plan states set and enforce standards, such as the HAZWOPER and Respiratory Protection standards, which are identical to or "at least as effective as" Federal OSHA standards, and therefore may have more stringent or supplemental requirements. EPA's parallel HAZWOPER Standard was adopted to cover emergency responders who would not be covered by the OSHA standard, including volunteers who work for a governmental agency engaged in emergency response, such as firefighters. For consistency, OSHA interprets the HAZWOPER Standard for the EPA. Federal OSHA administers the safety and health program for the private sector in the remaining states and territories, and also retains authority with regard to safety and health conditions for Federal employees throughout the nation.

DOCUMENT CONTENT AND ORGANIZATION

This best practices document (1) provides information to assist hospitals in selecting personal protective equipment (PPE) based on current interpretations of OSHA standards, published literature, current hospital practices, stakeholder input, and the practical limitations of currently available respiratory protective devices and (2) consolidates OSHA standards and interpretations on training needs of first receivers. These best practices build on health and safety programs that hospitals already should have in place under existing OSHA regulations (such as those listed in Updating Emergency Management Plans at page 32).

The section immediately following the introduction addresses details concerning PPE selection. The way in which hospitals can use best practices and the rationale for OSHA's conclusion on first receiver respiratory protection, glove selection, and protective clothing are all covered under the section "Personal Protective Equipment." Conclusions regarding personal protective equipment draws on information concerning hazards likely encountered by first receivers and specifies a minimum level of PPE for protecting first receivers against such hazards (Table 3). Unless a community-specific hazard analysis identifies unique hazards that first receivers are reasonably anticipated to encounter and that require greater (or varied) PPE, an employer who meets the prerequisites detailed in Tables 1 and 2 for limiting exposure can choose to rely on the PPE identified in Table 3 to comply with relevant OSHA PPE standards. Of course, employers are not obligated to follow the guidance in Table 3; any employer can choose instead to perform an independent hazard assessment that is sufficient to identify the hazards that its employees are reasonably anticipated to encounter, and then select PPE adequate to protect its employees against such hazards. Information on training first receivers appears in the final section. It also contains a summary of first receiver training (Table 4).

The appendices provide examples, which might be useful to hospitals developing or upgrading *emergency management plans* (EMPs). Appendix A of this best practices document provides background information on how various aspects of a hospital's preparation, response, and recovery impact employee protection during hazardous substance emergencies. Appendices B, C, and D list additional information sources, while Appendices E through M offer examples of procedures and equipment used in some hospitals. OSHA offers these examples for informational purposes only and does not recommend one option over the many effective alternatives that exist.

OSHA recommends that this best practices document be used in conjunction with other available emergency preparedness information sources, such as those listed in Appendices C and D, and other references that may become available in the future. Footnotes indicating current Joint Commission on Accreditation of Healthcare Organizations (JCAHO) Standards for Emergency Management (which are further described in Section EC 1.4 of JCAHO's Comprehensive Accreditation Manual for Hospitals) appear at key points in the document. In publishing this document, it is OSHA's intent to provide useful information that will assist hospitals and other healthcare providers in taking appropriate steps to protect first receivers and other affected workers from exposure to chemical, biological, and radiological substances.

This document is based on presently available information as well as current occupational safety and health provisions and standards. Employers should modify their procedures as appropriate when additional, relevant information becomes available or when modifications to Occupational Safety and Health Act (OSH Act) or JCAHO standards necessitate revision. The OSH Act requires employers to comply with hazard-specific safety and health standards. In addition, pursuant to Section 5(a)(1), the General Duty Clause of the OSH Act, employers must provide their employees with a workplace free from recognized hazards likely to cause death or serious physical harm. This document incorporates existing applicable regulatory provisions as well as non-mandatory work practices and methods that may be implemented to further supplement employee protection against exposure to hazardous substances. OSHA has attempted to clearly distinguish between mandatory and recommended work practices/methods within this document. Where regulations establish performance criteria for compliance, this document attempts to provide specific guidance that employers may use to adequately protect employees and comply with these regulatory provisions. However, an alternative approach may be justified given specific workplace circumstances. This document does not enlarge or diminish an employer's obligations under the OSH Act.

Occupational Safety and Health Administration

PPE selection for first receivers has been a topic of significant discussion (Hick et al., 2003a; Barbera and Macintyre, 2003; CA EMSA, 2003b; ECRI, 2002). At the root of this discussion is the need for hospitals to provide adequate protection for the reasonably anticipated worst-case employee exposure scenario, despite having limited information regarding the nature of the substance with which victims may be contaminated (OSHA, 2002b). This lack of information challenges hospitals' abilities to conduct the hazard assessments on which PPE selection must be based.[12]

Despite many hospitals' strong interest in powered air-purifying respirators (PAPR) as a practical form of respiratory protection for first receivers in the Hospital Decontamination Zone, many knowledgeable sources avoid making specific PPE recommendations, but rather point out the advantages and disadvantages of the various options, or recommend *appropriate* PPE (JCAHO, 2001; Lehmann, 2002; Penn, 2002).[13] Others offer stronger opinions. CA EMSA (2003a) promotes the use of a multi-tiered approach to PPE. Burgess (1999), in an article published prior to more recent letters of interpretation specific to healthcare workers, indicates that OSHA requires Level B protection or self-contained breathing apparatus (SCBA) for unknown hazards, but points out there are substantial difficulties for healthcare workers who attempt to care for patients while wearing this type of equipment and also addresses the hazards of wearing SCBAs (e.g., slips, trips, falls, and overexertion, particularly for infrequent users). These sources demonstrate appropriate caution in the face of unknown contaminants of unknown concentration. However, OSHA believes that the substantial body of recent information on first receivers' actual experiences and probable exposure levels now allows more definitive guidance.

---

[12] Hazard assessments for PPE are required under OSHA's Personal Protective Equipment standard – General Requirements, 29 CFR 1910.132(d), or the equivalent State Plan standards.

[13] The *Hospital Decontamination Zone* includes any areas where the type and quantity of hazardous substance is unknown and where contaminated victims, contaminated equipment, or contaminated waste may be present. It is reasonably anticipated that employees in this zone might have exposure to contaminated victims, their belongings, equipment, or waste. This zone includes, but is not limited to, places where initial triage and/or medical stabilization of possibly contaminated victims occur, pre-decontamination waiting (staging) areas for victims, the actual decontamination area, and the post-decontamination victim inspection area. This area will typically end at the emergency department (ED) door. In other documents this zone is sometimes called the "Warm Zone."

To assist hospitals, this section provides information that employers can use to provide a level of PPE that reasonably can be expected to protect first receivers from a wide range of hazards. OSHA's PPE selection guidance applies when the hazardous substance is unknown and the possible exposure is strictly limited by: (1) the quantity of material associated with living victims; and (2) other specific conditions, policies, equipment, and procedures in place that will reduce employee exposure. These best practices are preceded by instructions for using the document and by a discussion of the information considered in developing OSHA's PPE selection.

USING OSHA'S BEST PRACTICES

Using OSHA's Rationale for PPE Selection and Hazard Assessment

In Tables 1, 2, and 3 of this document, OSHA outlines prerequisite conditions necessary to limit first receiver exposure to unknown hazardous substances and presents information that employers can use to provide adequate PPE for first receivers. The prerequisite conditions in the first two tables are designed to minimize the exposure of first receivers and form part of the basis for OSHA's rationale for the PPE selection listed in Table 3. By implementing those prerequisites, hospitals can reduce the exposures of their own first receivers. Hospitals may then use the discussion in this section in conducting the required hazard assessment, which must consider hazards unique to the community in which they are located. In rare situations, these employers will need to augment or modify the PPE specified in Table 3 to provide adequate protection against unique hazards identified in the community-specific hazard analysis. Of course, employers are not obligated to follow the guidance in Table 3; any employer can choose instead to perform an independent hazard assessment that is sufficient to identify the hazards that its employees are reasonably anticipated to encounter, and then select PPE adequate to protect its employees against such hazards.

Augmenting the PPE Selection to Address Specific Hazards Identified by the Hazard Vulnerability Analysis (HVA) and the Community

The best practices presented in this document indicate the **minimum** PPE that OSHA anticipates generally will be needed to protect first receivers faced with a wide range of unknown hazards (providing the prerequisite conditions in Tables 1 and 2 are met). However, as with any generalized protection, OSHA's PPE for first receivers offers more protection against some hazards than others. When a hospital determines that first receivers could reasonably anticipate encountering a specific known hazard, the hospital also must determine whether this generalized protection must be supplemented to more fully address that specific hazard.

Specifically, to finish the hazard assessment and PPE selection process, each hospital must consult its own complete and updated HVA (required by JCAHO), as well as additional information available from the community (e.g., the Local Emergency Planning Committees (LEPC)). JCAHO requires that hospitals also consider their anticipated roles and coordinate activities with other emergency response agencies and hospitals within the community. When these sources point to a *specific* substance or situation from which the hospital should protect its first receivers, the hospital must confirm that PPE selection provides effective protection against that hazard. In rare situations, the process of considering the HVA and community-specific information will identify ways the hospital must augment the PPE specified in Table 3 for unknown hazards in order to help ensure protection against specific known hazards (e.g., by tailoring glove selection to address an identified, specific hazard, or by stocking additional supplies, such as a specific respirator cartridge known to protect the user from an identified, specific hazard).

Hospitals must adopt a more *specialized* level of protection (such as air-supplied respirators) if the hospital's role, position in the community, or HVA indicates a higher level of protection is necessary (e.g., if the hospital will field a HAZMAT team or provide other services *at the release site*, if the hospital is adjacent to a hazardous chemical storage facility that could subject first receivers to an environment immediately dangerous to life and health (IDLH), or if the hospital is the site of the incident).

RATIONALE FOR OSHA'S PERSONAL PROTECTIVE EQUIPMENT BEST PRACTICES

The following discussion reviews existing OSHA regulations, letters of interpretation, and published literature relevant to the selection of PPE for healthcare workers receiving contaminated victims. OSHA's best practices on first receiver PPE appear at the end of this section in Tables 1, 2, and 3.

Respiratory Protection
Limited Quantity of Contaminant on Victims

A key factor supporting OSHA's PPE best practices is the limited amount of toxic substance to which first receivers might be exposed. Many recent sources note that the quantity of contaminant on victims is restricted. For example, OSHA has made a clear distinction between the site where a hazardous substance was released and hospital-based decontamination facilities (OSHA, 1992a, 2002a). This distinction is important because it helps define the maximum amount of contaminant to which healthcare workers might be exposed (i.e., the quantity of material on living victims and their possessions when they arrive at the hospital). Horton et al. (2003) stated that during victim decontamination procedures the hazard to healthcare workers is strictly from secondary exposure and "depends largely on the toxicity of the substance on the victims' hair, skin, and clothing; the concentration of the substance; and the duration of contact [first receivers have] with the victim."

The quantity of contaminant that healthcare workers might encounter can be dramatically less than the amount to which the victim was exposed or that was originally deposited on the victim. Gas or vapor releases can expose victims to toxic concentrations, but tend to evaporate and dissipate quickly. Georgopoulos et al. (2004) determined that 100 grams (approximately 4 ounces) of most moderately to highly volatile substances that might be sprayed on a victim during a mass casualty incident would evaporate within 5 minutes from the time the exposure occurred. Unless the substance release occurs immediately adjacent to a hospital, it is not anticipated that victims will be able to reach the hospital within that period of time, or the more realistic 10-minute period that Georgopoulos et al. (2004) used in the exposure model presented later in this section.[14] Horton et al. (2003) agree, stating that substances released as gas or vapor "are not likely to pose a secondary contamination risk" to first receivers. It is important to note, however, that limited exposure might be possible. In an isolated incident reviewed by these authors, unprotected healthcare workers experienced skin and respi-

---

[14] Georgopoulos et al. (2004) suggest that "recognition of an event, identification of transportation means, and transportation to a healthcare facility are not expected to take less than 5 minutes even under ideal circumstances." The 10-minute (approximate) lag time can be reasonably assumed during a mass casualty event involving chemical release, except in cases where the release occurs immediately adjacent to the hospital (e.g., at a chemical plant next door to the hospital).

OSHA
Occupational Safety and
Health Administration

ratory irritation from highly toxic volatile substances (chlorine gas) thought to have permeated victims' clothing.[15] While an environment that is immediately dangerous is possible, it is extremely unlikely that a living victim could create an IDLH environment at a receiving hospital, particularly if contaminated clothing is quickly removed and isolated, and the victim is treated and decontaminated in an area with adequate ventilation.

Removal of victim's clothing, or, better yet, decontamination of victims before they arrive at the hospital have a marked effect on the quantity of contaminant that first receivers encounter. Pre-hospital decontamination can eliminate the risk of secondary contamination (Horton et al., 2003). Removing contaminated clothing can reduce the quantity of contaminant associated with victims by an estimated 75 to 90 percent (Macintyre et al., 2000; Vogt, 2002; USACHPPM, 2003a).[16] To control unnecessary exposure, Hospital A promotes the use of prescribed procedures for first responders assisting victims to remove clothing. The clothing is cut away using blunt-nose shears to eliminate stretching, flapping, wringing, or excessive handling of fabric that might contribute to worker exposure (or additional victim exposure).

Showering with tepid water and a liquid soap with good surfactant properties is widely considered an effective (and preferred) method for removing the remaining hazardous substance from victims' skin and hair (Goozner et al, 2002; Macintyre et al., 2000).[17] The U.S. Army promotes this method for chemicals (both chemical weapons and toxic industrial chemicals), radiological particles, and biological agents (USACHPPM, 2003a).[18] In several cases involving secondary exposure incidents reviewed by Horton et al. (2003), contaminated victims who caused injury to

healthcare workers were subsequently decontaminated. No further injury to healthcare workers was mentioned. See Procedures at page 43 for additional discussion of decontamination procedures for unknown contaminants. When the nature of the contaminant is known, the hospital can adjust the decontamination procedures to best remove the specific hazard.

As a final step in minimizing first receiver exposure to hazardous substances, the accepted industrial hygiene practice is for the healthcare workers also to shower following contact with contaminated victims and cleanse equipment as part of decontamination procedures. Hospital A uses a strict protocol for personnel to decontaminate themselves while removing gloves, protective suits, boots, and hooded powered air-purifying respirators (PAPRs). Hospital C includes decontamination of the shower system and associated equipment as part of those procedures.

Hospital Experience with Contaminated Victims

Several studies have reviewed public data and reports regarding victims of hazardous materials emergencies and associated secondary contamination of healthcare workers. First receivers rarely reported adverse health effects. Those workers who experienced symptoms were unprotected and tended to have close, extended contact with the contaminated victims. Horton et al. (2003) evaluated data from the Agency for Toxic Substances and Disease Registry (ATSDR) Hazardous Substance Emergency Events Surveillance (HSEES) system. Through 2001, the database had captured information on over 44,000 hazardous materials events involving substances other than petroleum products.[19] Although overall, healthcare workers were the 11th most common group injured in hazardous materials incidents, Horton determined that events affecting emergency department (ED) personnel appear to occur infrequently, representing only 0.2

---

[15] This incident is described in Horton et al. (2003) as part of an evaluation of hazardous materials incident data captured by the Agency for Toxic Substances and Disease Registry (ATSDR) Hazardous Substance Emergency Events Surveillance (HSEES) system.

[16] The percentage of contaminant reduction depends on the type of clothing the victim was wearing when exposed. The estimates may be somewhat lower (down to 50 percent) for victims wearing short pants or skirts and higher (up to 94 percent) for victims exposed to biological warfare agents while wearing protective military uniforms (USACHPPM, 2003a).

[17] Many liquid soaps have good surfactant properties (ability to cut grease) and are not excessively harsh on skin (e.g., major brands of hand dishwashing soap, such as Joy, Ivory, Dawn, and others, as well as shampoos). This is the method used by all seven hospitals interviewed for this project and is reportedly effective for all but the most tenacious substances. For example, the chemical weapon agent VX is difficult to wash from skin.

---

[18] A related practice of spraying a 0.5 percent solution of hypochlorite (equivalent to a 10 percent solution of Chlorox® household bleach) may have value for deactivating biological agents, other than mycotoxins, and some chemical weapons agents (mustard gas, organophosphates) if left in contact for a period of time (15 to 20 minutes). The solution might be used to decontaminate facilities, but is no longer considered an optimal or necessary treatment for human skin (Macintyre et al., 2000). Sources agree that there is no substantive difference in decontamination methods for biological and chemical agents.

[19] Using information from the 16 states that participated between 1995 and 2001, these authors determined that of the 44,045 hazardous materials events reported, 2,562 events (5.8 percent) involved victims who were transported to a hospital. Injuries to ED employees at the hospital were reported for six of these 2,562 events (0.2 percent).

percent of the 2,562 HSEES events in which victims were transported to a hospital.[20] Horton et al. (2003) also note that among the ED personnel injured, none wore any form of protection at the time of the injury. Respiratory tract and eye irritation were the primary symptoms and no employees required hospitalization.

A separate survey of ED evacuations at hospitals in the state of Washington also found a low incidence of secondary contamination of ED staff. Over a 5-year period, 101 hospitals reported only two evacuation incidents that also involved secondary contamination of staff, while ED evacuations due to hazardous substance incidents (usually caused by releases within the hospital) occurred 11 times.[21] The victims were not decontaminated prior to arrival at the hospital in either of the cases involving secondary contamination to staff (Burgess, 1999).

Walter et al. (2003) also reviewed municipal records to characterize hazardous materials responses. These authors evaluated all fire department hazardous materials reports, along with the associated emergency medical services encounter forms and hospital records for a mid-size metropolitan area (population 400,000). More than 70 percent of the hazardous materials incidents involved flammable materials (e.g., methane gas, diesel fuel, gasoline, and hydraulic oils), all of relatively low toxicity. Approximately 7 percent of the incidents involved highly toxic materials, all of which fell into the categories of mercury, pesticides, and cyanides. An additional 5 percent of the events were associated with toxic gases (primarily carbon monoxide, with a few cases of anhydrous ammonia or chlorine exposure). Corrosive materials accounted for another 10 percent of the incidents and primarily involved mineral acids and basic materials such as lime and sodium hydroxide.[22] Walter found that those patients transported to the hospital were usually treated for inhalation exposure to airborne toxicants, for which few required hospitalization. These findings

may explain the results of Horton et al. (2003) and Burgess (1999) who, as previously noted, identified few injuries among healthcare workers who treated victims of hazardous materials incidents. Victims exposed to gases or vapors are not anticipated to be contaminated with substantial quantities of these materials upon arrival at the hospital.

Hick et al. (2003a) reviewed the published literature and some individual case reports to assess the risk of contaminated patients to healthcare workers in the U.S. and abroad. These cases included incidents in which healthcare workers were exposed to secondary contamination, generally for periods of less than one hour.[23] Hick et al. (2003a) concluded that "...a contaminated patient presenting at the ED poses a definite health risk to providers. However, *even without personal protective equipment*, the risks of significant injury appear to be low, as reflected in this review and analysis of published cases." These authors found that the more serious injuries to healthcare workers are frequently associated with organophosphate compounds (e.g., sarin and certain pesticides), which are "extremely toxic, prone to off-gassing, and might have prolonged clinical effects...." The affected healthcare workers identified by the authors rarely used PPE.

Okumura et al. (1996) reported on the 1995 Tokyo subway sarin attack, in which one hospital received 640 victims (80 percent self-referred), 107 of whom were moderately injured and five were considered severely injured. Hick et al. (2003a) also reviewed the literature describing this incident and noted that more than 100 healthcare providers in Tokyo experienced symptoms (e.g., blurred vision) while treating victims. Of these, the most affected were several physicians who spent up to 40 minutes attempting to resuscitate the initial victims of the incident. The victims had *not* been decontaminated. These and other worker exposures were attributed to the failure of healthcare providers to use PPE and the practice of placing still-clothed, contaminated victims in a poorly ventilated waiting area.

It is interesting to note that although sarin (a notorious chemical warfare agent) affected many of the healthcare providers, all exposed providers at one of the primary receiving hospitals were reportedly able to continue their duties (Okumura et al., 1996). In the

---

[20] ED personnel accounted for about half of all healthcare workers injured. Other healthcare workers in the group included medical examiners in an autopsy room, coroner's assistants, a hospital worker at a highway rest area, and hospital employees injured when substances such as xylene and formalin were released in the hospital ("injuries were not the result of secondary contamination").

[21] This study only evaluated information on incidents that caused ED evacuation and did not consider other incidents that might have involved contaminated patients. The actual number of ED evacuation incidents may have been slightly higher due to under-reporting.

[22] Hazardous substances in miscellaneous categories accounted for the remainder of the reported incidents.

---

[23] Secondary exposures in the studies reviewed by Hick et al. (2003a) involved substances such as organophosphates (including sarin), hydrofluoric acid, pepper spray, chlorine gas, mixed solvents from methamphetamine laboratories, ethyldichlorosilane, and aluminum phosphide.

Tokyo terrorism incident, although victims' clothing was not removed and continued to be a source of contamination, *unprotected* first receivers experienced only limited exposures.[24] It is reasonable to anticipate that healthcare worker exposures might have been dramatically reduced by a combination of removing victims contaminated clothing, improving ventilation in patient waiting areas, and using PPE.

Exposure Modeling

Two studies conducted modeling of various phases of the victim disrobing and decontamination process in order to characterize first receiver exposure levels and evaluate the need for respiratory protection. These studies point out the need for a carefully developed and implemented EMP that includes hazard-reducing work practices, appropriate respiratory protection, and full body protection. In the first study, Schultz et al. (1995) collected air samples in the breathing zone of two healthcare workers during decontamination activities.[25] The test took place in an unventilated room, where the workers removed the simulated non-ambulatory patients' clothing and cleaned the skin using dry brushing to remove particles.[26]

The test periods included 5 minutes with the victim resting on a decontamination cart (to simulate a delay in clothing removal and decontamination), 2.5 minutes during which the healthcare workers cut away victims' clothing and placed it in a sealed container, and approximately 3 minutes of simulated skin cleaning. This latter activity generated visible dust during particulate trials.[27] The solvents evaporated completely during the 10-minute test periods and victim cleaning was not required for these agents. Healthcare worker exposure levels for dust ranged from 1.98 to 4.28 milligrams per cubic meter of air (mg/m3), while results for p-xylene ranged from 18 to 148 parts per million (ppm) and acetone concentrations were 185 to 459 ppm. The authors concluded that exposure levels were statistically lower than the applicable short-term exposure limits for these moderately toxic industrial chemicals; however, due to the uncertainties of hazardous materials management, "use of respiratory protective equipment should be continued."

In contrast to Schultz et al. (1995), which evaluated an industrial chemical of moderate toxicity, Georgopoulos et al. (2004) used a probability model to predict the level of respiratory protection that decontamination hospital staff would require to limit their exposure to several highly toxic industrial chemicals (chlorine, phosgene, and cyanide) and chemical weapons agents (nerve and blister agents). The model takes into account the substance's relative toxicity, vapor pressure, and dispersion characteristics, as well as the probable amount and distribution of contaminant on the victim, and the amount of time the substance would require to evaporate from the victim. The model also considered the number of victims, the length of time between the victims' exposure and arrival at the hospital, atmospheric conditions, and how soon after arrival the victims' contaminated clothing can be removed. Using Monte Carlo analysis and parameters set to consider *extreme* worst-case scenarios, the authors concluded that if contaminated clothing remains an ongoing source of contamination over a period of 6 hours of *constant* exposure, less than 2 percent of healthcare workers would be exposed to levels of sarin that would exceed the protection offered by a respirator providing at least 1,000-fold protection.[28] This percentage dropped when inputs associated with more likely scenarios were

---

[24] At a second Tokyo hospital, however, five of the most seriously exposed healthcare workers did require injection of antidote; although, they were able to continue to provide medical care (Nozaki et al., 1995).

[25] Investigators used an adult size plastic mannequin dressed in lightweight cotton clothing and contaminated with either an industrial solvent (800 milliliters [ml] acetone or p-xylene in multiple tests) or respirable size metal oxide particulates. The 800 ml represented the greatest amount of solvent the victim could bring to the room—that was the amount that completely saturated the clothes when placed in a container.

[26] The room measured 16 by 20 feet with a 10-foot ceiling and air temperature was reportedly 65° F.

[27] Macintyre et al. (2000) suggest vacuuming as an alternative to dry brushing victims contaminated with water-reactive dust.

[28] In this study, parameters for initial modeling of the maximum exposure that can reasonably be expected in a terrorist attack included a distribution of between 10 and 100 grams of chemical agent deposited over a mean of 1 square meter of surface area on 20 to 25 percent of the victims; lag time from initial dissemination of the agent to arrival of the victim at the hospitals represented with both truncated normal and an exponential distribution (mean value of 10 minutes); an air flow velocity distribution with a mean of 60 meters per minute across the victim, with chemical agent mixing occurring in an air column of 1 square meter cross-sectional area; and each first receiver directly participating constantly in a six-hour decontamination process. The healthcare worker was considered protected if the dose the worker would receive during 6 hours of continuous decontamination activity was less than the value of 2.1 mg-min/m3 for sarin. This concentration is the equivalent of the 60-minute National Research Council Acute Exposure Guideline Levels (AEGL-2) for sarin of 0.035 mg/m3 (multiplied by 60 minutes) (USACHPPM, 2003b). The Georgopoulos study shows that some transient effects and impairment might occur, but permanent health effects are highly unlikely.

used (e.g., increased evaporation transfer rate or increased lag time before the victim reached the hospital). Furthermore, related analysis showed that *if contaminated clothing is removed immediately when the victim arrives* at the hospital, "the level of sarin exposure to a healthcare worker would be negligible" and adequate protection would be provided by air purifying respirators with an assigned protection factor (APF) of 1,000.[29]

If correctly selected, fitted, used, and maintained, respiratory protective equipment reduces significantly the effective exposure level that an employee experiences. An employee wearing a respirator that offers a protection factor of 1,000 will breathe air that contains no more than 1/1,000 (or 0.1 percent) of the contaminant level outside the respirator. OSHA recently proposed an APF of 1,000 for certain designs of hood/helmet respirators.[30, 31] Full facepiece and hood/helmet supplied air respirators (excluding loose-fitting facepieces) are also assigned an APF of 1,000 in the proposed rule (Federal Register, 2003 (68 FR 34035)).[32]

The combination of high efficiency (HE) particulate filters plus organic vapor (OV) cartridges currently available for PAPRs will protect against many of the airborne hazards that first receivers might encounter (e.g., toxic dusts, biological agents, radioactive particulates, organophosphates and other pesticides, and solvents). Acid gas cartridges add an additional level of protection from gases such as chlorine, which generally will dissipate before victims arrive at the hospital, but which have been implicated in at least one case of healthcare worker injury.[33] It is not anticipated that first receivers would benefit from cartridges that

remove carbon monoxide from air. Despite the number of carbon monoxide victims treated at hospitals, there are no reported cases of healthcare workers being injured through secondary contamination from victims of carbon monoxide poisoning (Horton et al., 2003; Hick et al, 2003a; Walter et al., 2003).

As an applied example, Hospital A used some of these modeling techniques to complement a detailed HVA, a comprehensive staff training program, and a detailed EMP that makes safety and exposure reduction strong priorities.[34] This modeling allowed Hospital A to determine that there was not a need for respiratory protection greater than a hooded powered air purifying respirator [PAPR], fitted with high efficiency dust, organic vapor, and acid gas cartridges. The hospital determined that employees need to be protected from skin contact with the contaminant. Thus, individuals involved in decontaminating victims at this hospital wear PAPRs, splash-resistant suits, a double layer of gloves, and chemical-protective boots. Openings to the suits are closed with tape to create a barrier.

Gloves and Boots

No single glove or boot material will protect against every substance. Most glove manufacturers offer detailed guides to glove materials and their chemical resistance. Butyl rubber gloves generally provide better protection than nitrile gloves for chemical warfare agents and most toxic industrial chemicals that are more likely to be involved in a terrorist incident, although the converse applies to some industrial chemicals. Foil-based gloves are highly resistant to a wide variety of hazardous substances and could also be considered when determining an appropriate protective ensemble. Hospitals must select materials that cover the specific substances that the hospital has determined first receivers reasonably might encounter. However, given the broad scope of potential contaminants, OSHA considers it of vital importance for hospitals also to select materials that protect against a wide range of substances. A double layer of gloves, made of two different materials, or foil-based gloves resist the broadest range of chemicals.

In general, the same material selected for gloves will also be appropriate for boots. Because boot walls tend to be thicker than gloves, boots of any material

---

[29] Sarin was selected for this model because it has a moderate vapor pressure (similar to water) and thus would not necessarily evaporate before the victim could reach the hospital. Additionally, the substance does off-gas to an extent that can cause injury to healthcare workers. Finally, among chemical substances with vapor pressures in this range, sarin was selected as the most toxic. For purposes of comparison, NIOSH (2003) publishes vapor pressure levels for numerous industrial chemicals.

[30] This provision is part of a proposed rule (68 FR 34035, June 6, 2003); the APF provisions that OSHA eventually develops may differ substantially from those in the proposed rule.

[31] Respirator manufacturers must be able to show test results indicating the respirator meets specified criteria.

[32] For comparison, a non-powered full facepiece air-purifying respirator has an APF of 50, while SCBA is assigned a protection factor of 10,000.

[33] The contaminant might have been trapped in victims' clothing (Horton et al., 2003). It is reasonable to anticipate that exposures would have been eliminated if the victim's clothing had been removed in a well-ventilated space (or outdoors) immediately upon arrival at the hospital.

[34] See the acknowledgments at the beginning of this document for a brief statement regarding the hospitals interviewed for this guidance.

are likely to be more protective than gloves of the same material.

A combination of gloves, for example, butyl gloves worn over inner nitrile gloves, are often the best option for use by hospital workers during emergencies and mass casualties involving hazardous substances. However, hospitals are advised to select the combination that best meet their specific needs.

Glove thickness is measured in mils, with a higher number of mils indicating a thicker glove. Using common examples, exam gloves are often approximately 4 mil, while general-purpose household (kitchen) gloves are 12–16 mil, and heavy industrial gloves might be 20 to 30 mil.

Depending on the dexterity needed by the hospital worker, the glove selection can be modified to allow for the use of a glove combination that is thinner than that usually recommended for the best protection. As an example, the U.S. Army Center for Health Promotion and Preventive Medicine (USACHPPM) recommends that hospital personnel working with victims potentially contaminated with chemical warfare agents or toxic industrial chemicals wear a combination of chemical protective gloves, such as butyl rubber gloves over inner nitrile gloves (USACHPPM, 2003a).[35] Because thicker gloves offer greater protection, USACHPPM recommends a butyl glove with a minimum thickness of 14 mil (over a 4 or 5 mil nitrile

glove). However, with increased thickness comes greater loss of manual dexterity. When advanced medical procedures must be performed before decontamination, thicker gloves might be too awkward, and, therefore, it might be necessary to use a butyl rubber glove of 7 mil over the nitrile glove, or a 14 mil butyl rubber glove alone (USACHPPM, 2003a). If sterility is required and decontamination is not possible before procedures, a double layer of disposable 4 to 5 mil nitrile gloves might be the best option (USACHPPM, 2003a). Not all sources recommend double gloves; for example, the U.S. Army Soldier and Biological Chemical Command's (SBCCOM) Domestic Preparedness Program (DPP) recommends butyl rubber gloves for personnel performing decontamination operations and casualty care (SBCCOM, 2000a). Among the sterile gloves readily available, those made of nitrile offer the best resistance to the widest range of substances (but not all). Note that thinner gloves deteriorate (tear and rip) more rapidly than thicker gloves. When thinner gloves must be used, they should be changed frequently.

Hendler et al. (2000), as cited in USACHPPM (2003a), conducted a study to determine the effect of full PPE (including 12-mil "tactile" gloves and a full facepiece mask) on intubation performance. Clinicians wearing this equipment could perform endotracheal intubation effectively (i.e., the tube was inserted in sufficient time), but the procedure did take longer than it would have without PPE. Intubation delays would cause subsequent decontamination procedures and medical treatment to be delayed by a corresponding amount of time.

Protective Garments

The optimal garment material for first receivers will protect against a wide range of chemicals in liquid, solid, or vapor form (phase). Because first receivers might become contaminated with liquid or solid (dust) contaminants through physical contact with a contaminated victim, the ideal fabric will repel chemicals during incidental contact (protection from gases is less important because, as shown earlier, gases generally will dissipate before a victim arrives at the hospital). Additionally, the optimal garment will restrict the passage of vapors, both through the suit fabric and through openings in the suit. Finally, optimal clothing is also sufficiently flexible, durable, and lightweight for long-term wear (up to several hours) during physically active work.

[35] SBCCOM tested several glove types. Results from two different studies are presented here as examples of the information available on breakthrough times. However, additional tests continue to be performed. Consult glove manufacturers for the most recent information. In their first study, SBCCOM tested eleven glove designs (including butyl, neoprene, and nitrile) for breakthrough times when exposed to concentrated Mustard (blister agent) or Sarin (nerve agent). Breakthrough times were dependent on material and thickness. A 30 mil Best Butyl glove had a breakthrough time of 810 minutes for Mustard and greater than 1440 minutes for Sarin. MAPA Neoprene gloves (mil not stated) had a breakthrough time of 298 minutes for Mustard and greater than 1440 minutes for Sarin. Ansell Edmont TNT Nitrile gloves [4 mil] had a breakthrough time of 20 minutes for Mustard and 106 minutes for Sarin. Ansell Edmont Sol-Vex (Nitrile) [15 mil] had a breakthrough time of 109 minutes for Mustard and greater than 1440 minutes for Sarin. Test data revealed that the chemical protective glove designs can protect wearers from liquid chemical warfare agents (SBCCOM, 2001a). In the second study, SBCCOM tested four glove designs (including butyl and nitrile) for breakthrough times when exposed to Mustard (blister agent) or Sarin (nerve agent). Breakthrough times were dependent on material and thickness. N-Dex Disposable Nitrile gloves (4 mil) had a breakthrough time of 53 minutes for Mustard and 51 minutes for Sarin. North Butyl gloves (20 mil) had a breakthrough time of greater than 1440 minutes for both Mustard and Sarin. Test data revealed that the chemical protective glove designs can protect wearers from liquid chemical warfare agents (SBCCOM, 2001b).

Manufacturers produce a variety of suit fabrics and designs, and several commercially available broad-spectrum protective fabrics might be appropriate, depending on the situations and hazards that the hospital anticipates first receivers reasonably might be expected to encounter. While OSHA does not test, endorse, or recommend specific products, examples of such products include: Tyvek® F, Tychem® CPF3, CPF4, Tychem® BR, Tychem® LV, Tychem® SL, Zytron® 100, Zytron® 200, Zytron® 300, Zytron® 400, Zytron® 500, and Zytron® 600, ProVent® 10,000, and DuraVent® 2.8. Before selecting materials, contact the manufacturer for specific application guidance.

Fabric and suit manufacturers can provide laboratory-testing information regarding specific materials. For example, Tyvek® F has been tested extensively by military organizations and accredited testing laboratories.[36] As another example, the SBCCOM DPP tested vapor-blocking properties of six different protective suits in a simulated, high-vapor environment. In the results tabulated below, the Tyvek® F suite (ProTech model) offered a protection factor of 42 (vapor levels outside the suit were 42 times higher than inside the suit), which was approximately twice the protection than was provided by the next best performing suits. Traditional Tyvek® (protection factor of 4) was twice as protective as a standard police uniform (protection factor of 2). These suits were tested by placing sensors for the test vapor under the suits at 17 specific body locations. Volunteers wore the protective gear while performing the activities normally associated with an actual *first responder* chemical response (but did not involve physical acts, such as patient handling, that would likely be required of first receivers) (SBCCOM, 2003).

Figure 1. Results of Simulation Tests on Several Chemical Suits

Suit Configuration	# Suits Tested	Protection Factor
Standard [Police] Uniform	2	2
Tyvek® Protective Wear Suit	4	4
Tychem® 9400 Protective Suit	4	17
Kappler® CPF4 Protective Suit	4	18
Tychem® SL Protective Suit	5	24
Tyvek® ProTech F Protective Suit	5	42

(Source: SBCCOM, 2003)

The ability of protective garment fabric to withstand physical abrasion and tearing is also important. When assisting non-ambulatory victims, first receivers might subject the protective garments to physical stresses that should be considered in garment selection. The National Fire Protection Association (NFPA) in *NFPA Standard No. 1994 on Protective Ensemble for Chemical/Biological Terrorism Incidents* offers criteria for evaluating performance of protective garments, including detailed specifications for bursting, puncture, and tear resistance, as well as garment seam specifications (NFPA, 2001). [Editorial note: Previous versions of this Best Practices document made specific reference to NFPA 1994 Classes 2 and 3. This reference has been removed.]

CONCLUSIONS REGARDING PERSONAL PROTECTIVE EQUIPMENT

Evidence in the U.S. and abroad shows that unprotected healthcare workers can be injured by secondary exposure to hazardous substances when they treat contaminated patients. However, OSHA concludes that hospitals that make a conscientious effort can limit the secondary exposure of healthcare workers to a level at which chemical protective clothing (including gloves, boots, and garments with openings taped closed) and PAPRs will provide adequate protection from a wide range of hazardous substances to which first receivers most likely could be exposed. This conclusion is based on the infrequency with which healthcare workers have been affected (despite the numerous hazardous substance incidents), the experiences of hospitals treating contaminated victims, the nature of the injuries healthcare workers sustain when they are affected (during both acts of terrorism and accidental releases), and the exposure models described above. OSHA believes that the 1,000-fold protection factor that has been attained by

---

[36] Independent accredited testing laboratories conducted permeation tests on Tyvek® F for Dupont. The breakthrough times for the chemical warfare agents, Mustard, Tabun, Sarin, Soman, and VX, exceeded 720 minutes. The breakthrough time for Lewisite was 360 minutes. The breakthrough times for industrial chemicals of special concern, Chlorine, Formaldehyde (Formalin solution), Hydrochloric Acid (37%), and Concentrated Sulfuric Acid was greater than 480 minutes. The breakthrough time for Ammonia was 79 minutes, for Ethylene Oxide 65 minutes, for Fuming Nitric Acid 14 minutes, for Sulfur Dioxide 38 minutes, and for Hydrogen Fluoride permeation was immediate (DuPont, 2003). Additionally, TNO Laboratories in the Netherlands tested and certified Tyvek® F, having passed all the standard North American Treaty Organization (NATO) tests for chemical warfare protection (DuPont, 2002).

certain PAPRs in simulated workplace conditions, in combination with protective gloves, boots, and garments with openings taped closed, will be adequate to protect first receivers who are decontaminating victims.[37] Government experts, researchers, and hospitals alike offer broad support for the use of PAPRs and chemical protective clothing (including gloves, boots, and suits with the openings taped closed) for first receivers performing decontamination activities (Hick et al., 2003a; Georgopoulos et al., 2004; Macintyre et al., 2000; MMWR, 2001). Furthermore, OSHA believes the decontamination process itself, along with adequate employee training, will prevent injury to ED staff working in the Hospital Post-decontamination Zone.[38]

Based on information gathered from a wide variety of sources, OSHA has concluded that the PPE specified in Table 3 will provide adequate protection for first receivers exposed to unknown hazardous substances in most circumstances. Although applicable to a wide range of hospitals, the guidance in Table 3 for minimum first receiver PPE is conditional – to limit first receiver exposures to levels at which the PPE specified in Table 3 will provide effective protection, hospitals must meet the specified prerequisite conditions of eligibility set forth in Tables 1 and 2. Employers who meet the prerequisites in Tables 1 and 2 may use this best practices document as the OSHA-required generalized hazard assessment. Such employers may choose to rely on the PPE specified in Table 3 to comply with relevant OSHA standards and to provide effective protection for first receivers against a wide range of hazardous substances. However, such employers also must conduct a hazard assessment that considers hazards unique to the community in which they are located. In rare situations, these employers will need to augment or modify the PPE specified in Table 3 to provide adequate protection against unique hazards identified in the community-specific hazard analysis. Of course, employers are not obligated to follow the guidance in Table 3; any employer can choose instead to perform an independent hazard assessment that is sufficient to identify the hazards that its employees are reasonably anticipated to encounter, and then select PPE adequate to protect its employees against such hazards.

OSHA believes that hospitals are becoming increasingly prepared for mass casualty incidents involving unidentified hazardous substances. As a result, OSHA anticipates that many (and eventually most) hospitals will meet the conditions in Tables 1 and 2 that will help them manage secondary exposures such that employees can be effectively protected when using the first receiver PPE presented in Table 3. Recent incidents (including the World Trade Center and anthrax attacks) and current JCAHO requirements provide hospitals with strong incentive to take the necessary steps to prepare themselves and their staff to function safely during mass casualty incidents involving hazardous substance releases. Many of the JCAHO requirements help hospitals better identify the actual conditions that they might face in an emergency, which in turn allows the hospitals to make realistic plans for managing emergencies in a way that minimizes the risk to employees. The JCAHO requirements, along with the hospital's commitment to maintaining JCAHO accreditation and OSHA compliance, provide the basis for conducting detailed HVAs, identifying the hospital's role in the community, coordinating plans with other organizations, conducting drills to test all phases of preparedness, training personnel, and implementing PPE and respiratory protection programs. The additional exposure-limiting conditions, such as removing and safely containing contaminated clothing and other personal items as soon as victims arrive at the hospital, are primarily procedural and can be addressed through standard operating procedures and clear communication with victims and hospital staff.

OSHA concludes that PAPRs with helmet/hoods are a practical choice for first receivers. Helmet/hood PAPRs require no fit testing, can be worn by employees with facial hair and eyeglasses, and are generally considered by most workers to be more comfortable than negative pressure APRs (see also Appendix E for a comparison of the relative advantages of various facepiece styles).[39] Hospitals that take the steps outlined in Tables 1 and 2 will limit the exposures of first receivers to a level against which PAPRs will normally offer suitable protection. Other respirators that provide an APF of 1,000 or higher are also alternatives.

OSHA recommends PAPRs to ensure the appropriate level of protection for situations when the haz-

---

[37] In a 2003 Federal Register entry, OSHA proposed an APF of 1,000 for some models of PAPR (68 FR 34035, June 6, 2003).

[38] The *Hospital Post-decontamination Zone* is an area considered uncontaminated. Equipment and personnel are not expected to become contaminated in this area. At a hospital receiving contaminated victims, the Hospital Post-decontamination Zone includes the ED (unless contaminated). In other documents this zone is sometimes called the "Cold Zone."

---

[39] Tight-fitting respirators do require fit testing.

ardous substance is unknown and unquantified. Non-powered APRs have a role in protecting first receivers when the hazardous substance has been identified and quantified. First receivers may use such respirators after accurate information confirms that a negative pressure respirator will adequately protect the wearer from the identified inhalation hazard.

Any respiratory protection for first receivers must be included in a formal written respiratory protection program, as required by 29 CFR 1910.134 (Respiratory Protection), or the parallel State Plan standards. Hospitals can integrate the respirators into their existing respiratory protection program, which must include the following elements:

- Procedures for selecting respirators for use in the workplace.
- Medical evaluations of employees required to use respirators.
- Fit testing procedures for tight-fitting respirators.
- Procedures for proper use of respirators in routine and reasonably anticipated scenarios.
- Procedures and schedules for cleaning, disinfecting, storing, inspecting, repairing, discarding, and otherwise maintaining respirators.
- Procedures for establishing and implementing respirator chemical cartridge change schedules.
- Procedures to ensure adequate air quality, quantity, and flow of breathing air for atmosphere-supplying respirators.
- Training of employees in the respiratory hazards to which they are potentially exposed during routine and emergency situations.

First Receiver Hospital Decontamination Zones

OSHA has found it appropriate to define two functional zones during hospital-based decontamination activities. These zones, which guide the application of OSHA's recommendations, are:

- Hospital Decontamination Zone
- Hospital Post-decontamination Zone

The *Hospital Decontamination Zone* includes any areas where the type and quantity of hazardous substance is unknown and where contaminated victims, contaminated equipment, or contaminated waste may be present. It is reasonably anticipated that employees in this zone might have exposure to contaminated victims, their belongings, equipment, or waste. This zone includes, but is not limited to, places where ini-

tial triage and/or medical stabilization of possibly contaminated victims occur, pre-decontamination waiting (staging) areas for victims, the actual decontamination area, and the post-decontamination victim inspection area. This area will typically end at the ED door. In other documents this zone is sometimes called the "Warm Zone."

The Hospital Post-decontamination Zone is an area considered uncontaminated. Equipment and personnel are not expected to become contaminated in this area. At a hospital receiving contaminated victims, the Hospital Post-decontamination Zone includes the ED (unless contaminated). In other documents this zone is sometimes called the "Cold Zone."

PPE Table and Tables Listing Prerequisite Conditions for Specified PPE

The following pages contain three tables. The first two, Tables 1 and 2, list steps that hospitals must take or conditions that must exist before relying upon the PPE specified in Table 3. These steps and conditions help limit employee exposures and are necessary to ensure that the PPE for both zones listed in Table 3 will adequately protect employees. In other words, OSHA has determined that the minimum first receiver PPE outlined in Table 3 should protect healthcare workers as they care for contaminated victims of mass casualty incidents within the two zones; however, hospitals need to meet certain exposure-limiting conditions (outlined in Tables 1 and 2) to ensure that employees are adequately protected from all reasonably foreseeable hazards. Many hospitals can, or will soon be able to, meet these conditions, many of which parallel existing JCAHO and OSHA (OSHA-approved State Plan) requirements. These PPE best practices are applicable to all hospitals that might receive victims contaminated with unknown substances; however, hospitals must complete the hazard assessment process and tailor the PPE selection to also address specific hazards they might reasonably be anticipated to encounter. Additionally, some hospitals may determine that an alternative mix of PPE is appropriate for their particular situations. These options include using more protective PPE (to perform specialized activities or when conditions in Tables 1 and 2 cannot be met), or conducting an independent hazard assessment to support an alternative PPE selection.

Table 1. Hospital Decontamination Zone
Conditions Necessary for Hospitals to Rely on the
Personal Protective Equipment (PPE) Selection Presented in Table 3[A,B]

1. Thorough and complete hazard vulnerability analysis (HVA) and emergency management plan (EMP), which consider community input, have been conducted/developed, and have been updated within the past year.

2. The EMP includes plans to assist the numbers of victims that the community anticipates might seek treatment at this hospital, keeping in mind that the vast majority of victims may self-refer to the nearest hospital.

3. Preparations specified in the EMP have been implemented (e.g., employee training, equipment selection, maintenance, and a respiratory protection program).

4. The EMP includes methods for handling the numbers of ambulatory and non-ambulatory victims anticipated by the community.

5. The hazardous substance was not released in close proximity to the hospital, and the lapse time between the victims' exposure and victims' arrival at the hospital exceeds approximately 10 minutes, thereby permitting substantial levels of gases and vapors from volatile substances time to dissipate.[C]

6. Victims' contaminated clothing and possessions are promptly removed and contained (e.g., in an approved hazardous waste container that is isolated outdoors), and decontamination is initiated promptly upon arrival at the hospital. Hospital EMP includes shelter, tepid water, soap, privacy, and coverings to promote victim compliance with decontamination procedures.

7. EMP procedures are in place to ensure that contaminated medical waste and waste water do not become a secondary source of employee exposure.

And

8. The decontamination system and pre-decontamination victim waiting areas are designed and used in a manner that promotes constant fresh air circulation through the system to limit hazardous substance accumulation.[D] Air exchange from a clean source has been considered in the design of fully enclosed systems (i.e., through consultation with a professional engineer or certified industrial hygienist) and air is not re-circulated.

[A] The *Hospital Decontamination Zone* includes any areas where the type and quantity of hazardous substance is unknown and where contaminated victims, contaminated equipment, or contaminated waste may be present. It is reasonably anticipated that employees in this zone might have exposure to contaminated victims, their belongings, equipment, or waste. This zone includes, but is not limited to, places where initial triage and/or medical stabilization of possibly contaminated victims occur, pre-decontamination waiting (staging) areas for victims, the actual decontamination area, and the post-decontamination victim inspection area. This area will typically end at the emergency department (ED) door. In other documents this zone is sometimes called the "Warm Zone."

[B] Hospitals that do not meet these conditions must use more protective PPE or conduct a detailed hazard assessment to support a different selection.

[C] Note: Georgopoulos et al. (2004) suggest that "recognition of an event, identification of transportation means, and transportation to a healthcare facility are not expected to take less than 5 minutes even under ideal circumstances." The 10-minute (approximate) lag time can be reasonably assumed during a mass casualty event involving chemical release, except in cases where the release occurs immediately adjacent to the hospital (e.g., at a chemical factory next door to the hospital). This number of minutes is approximate and intended to provide guidance regarding what might be considered "immediately adjacent."

[D] Georgopoulos et al. (2004) recommend using fans to provide air movement.

Table 2. Hospital Post-decontamination Zone

Conditions Necessary for Hospitals to Rely on the

Personal Protective Equipment (PPE) Selection Presented in Table 3[E,F]

1. Emergency management plan (EMP) is developed and followed in a way that minimizes the emergency department (ED) personnel's reasonably anticipated contact with contaminated victims (e.g., with drills that test communication between the hospital and emergency responders at the incident site to reduce the likelihood of unanticipated victims).

2. Decontamination system (in the Hospital Decontamination Zone) and hospital security can be activated promptly to minimize the chance that victims will enter the ED and contact unprotected staff prior to decontamination.

3. EMP procedures specify that unannounced victims (once identified as possibly contaminated) disrobe in the appropriate decontamination area (not the ED) and follow hospital decontamination procedures before admission (or re-admission) to the ED.

4. Victims in this area were previously decontaminated by a shower with soap and water, including a minimum of 5 minutes under running water. Shower instructions are clearly presented and enforced. Shower facility encourages victim compliance (e.g., shelter, tepid water, reasonable degree of privacy).

5. EMP procedures clearly specify actions ED clerks or staff will take if they suspect a patient is contaminated. For example: (1) do not physically contact the patient, (2) immediately notify supervisor and safety officer of possible hospital contamination, and (3) allow qualified personnel to isolate and decontaminate the victim.

And

6. The EMP requires that if the ED becomes contaminated, that space is no longer eligible to be considered a Hospital Post-decontamination Zone. Instead, it should be considered contaminated and all employees working in this area should use PPE as described for the Hospital Decontamination Zone (see Table 3).

[E] The *Hospital Post-decontamination Zone* is an area considered uncontaminated. Equipment and personnel are not expected to become contaminated in this area. At a hospital receiving contaminated victims, the Hospital Post-decontamination Zone includes the ED (unless contaminated). In other documents this zone is sometimes called the "Cold Zone."

[F] Hospitals that do not meet these conditions must use more protective PPE or conduct a detailed hazard assessment to support a different selection.

Table 3. Minimum Personal Protective Equipment (PPE)
for Hospital-based First Receivers of Victims from Mass Casualty Incidents
Involving the Release of Unknown Hazardous Substances

SCOPE AND LIMITATIONS

This Table applies when:
- The hospital is not the release site.[G]
- The identity of the hazardous substance is unknown.[H]
- Prerequisite conditions of hospital eligibility are already met (Tables 1 and 2).

Note: This table is part of, and intended to be used with, the document entitled *OSHA Best Practices for Hospital-based First Receivers of Victims from Mass Casualty Incidents Involving the Release of Hazardous Substances.*

ZONE	MINIMUM PPE
Hospital Decontamination Zone[I] • All employees in this zone (Includes, but not limited to, any of the following employees: decontamination team members, clinicians, set-up crew, cleanup crew, security staff, and patient tracking clerks.)	• Powered air-purifying respirator (PAPR) that provides a protection factor of 1,000.[J] The respirator must be NIOSH-approved.[K] • Combination 99.97% high-efficiency particulate air (HEPA)/organic vapor/acid gas respirator cartridges (also NIOSH-approved). • Double layer protective gloves.[L] • Chemical resistant suit. • Head covering and eye/face protection (if not part of the respirator). • Chemical-protective boots. • Suit openings sealed with tape.
Hospital Post-decontamination Zone[M] • All employees in this zone	• Normal work clothes and PPE, as necessary, for infection control purposes (e.g., gloves, gown, appropriate respirator).

[G] When the hospital is not the release site, the quantity of contaminant is limited to the amount associated with the victims.

[H] If a hospital is specifically responding to a known hazard, the hospital must ensure that the selected PPE adequately protects the employees from the identified hazard. Thus, hospitals must augment or modify the PPE in Table 3 if the specified PPE is not sufficient to protect employees from the identified hazard. Alternatively, if a hazard assessment demonstrates that the specified PPE is not necessary to effectively protect workers from the identified hazard, a hospital would be justified in selecting less protective PPE, as long as the PPE actually selected by the hospital provides effective protection against the hazard.

[I] The *Hospital Decontamination Zone* includes any areas where the type and quantity of hazardous substance is unknown and where contaminated victims, contaminated equipment, or contaminated waste may be present. It is reasonably anticipated that employees in this zone might have exposure to contaminated victims, their belongings, equipment, or waste. This zone includes, but is not limited to, places where initial triage and/or medical stabilization of possibly contaminated victims occur, pre-decontamination waiting (staging) areas for victims, the actual decontamination area, and the post-decontamination victim inspection area. This area will typically end at the emergency department (ED) door.

[J] OSHA recently proposed an assigned protection factor (APF) of 1,000 for certain designs of hood/helmet-style PAPRs (Federal Register, 2003). An OSHA memorandum, which provides interim guidance pending the conclusion of the APF rule-

making, listed several PAPR hood/helmet respirators that are treated as having an APF of 1,000 for protection against particulates in the pharmaceutical industry (OSHA, 2002c (Memo for RAs)). The American National Standards Institute (ANSI), in Standard Z88.2 on Respiratory Protection, also indicates an APF of 1,000 for certain PAPRs. A hooded-style PAPR provides greater skin protection, has greater user acceptance, and does not require fit testing under 29 CFR 1910.134, thus might be preferred over a tight-fitting respirator. However, a tight-fitting full facepiece PAPR might offer more protection in the event of PAPR battery failure.

[K] Hospitals must use NIOSH-approved CBRN (chemical, biological, radiological, and nuclear) respirators, as they become available, when the HVA reveals a potential WMD threat. Until NIOSH completes its CBRN certification process for PAPRs, use PAPRs that have been tested by the manufacturer for a CBRN environment.

[L] Material for protective gloves, clothing, boots, and hoods must protect workers against the specific substances that they reasonably might be expected to encounter. However, given the broad range of potential contaminants, OSHA considers it vitally important that hospitals also select PPE that provides protection against a wide range of substances. No material will protect against all possible hazards.

[M] The *Hospital Post-decontamination Zone* is an area considered uncontaminated. Equipment and personnel are not expected to become contaminated in this area. At a hospital receiving contaminated victims, the Hospital Post-decontamination Zone includes the ED (unless contaminated).

The training indicated for first receivers depends on the individuals' roles and functions, the zones in which they work, and the likelihood that they will encounter contaminated patients.[41] OSHA recognizes that hospital staff who decontaminate victims at the hospital are removed from the site of the emergency (OSHA, 2002a, 2002b, 19992b). However, letters of interpretation provide that HAZWOPER First Responder Operations Level and First Responder Awareness Level training meet the requirements for first receivers in certain roles and positions. For other employees, a briefing at the time of the incident will be appropriate. In each case, the training must be effective, that is, be provided in a manner that the employee is capable of understanding.[42]

The following sections discuss HAZWOPER training provisions and contemplate levels of training commensurate with the employees' designated role within the EMP.

OPERATIONS LEVEL TRAINING

OSHA letters of interpretation specify that hospitals must provide HAZWOPER First Responder Operations Level training to first receivers who are expected to decontaminate victims or handle victims before they are thoroughly decontaminated (OSHA, 2003, 2002b, 1999, 1992c, 1991a). This level of training is appropriate for anyone with a designated role in the Hospital Decontamination Zone.

Training requirements for First Responder Operations Level appear under 29 CFR 1910.120 (q)(6)(ii), which indicates a minimum training duration of 8 hours and outlines topics to be covered (competencies the employee must acquire). Both the required competencies and training time were recently confirmed in an interpretive letter (OSHA, 2003). OSHA, however, allows these topics (but not the minimum training time) to be tailored to better meet the needs

of first responders. For example, the training might omit topics that are not directly relevant to the employee's role (e.g., recognition of Department of Transportation placards), but instead should include alternative training on hazard recognition (e.g., signs and symptoms of contamination or exposure), on decontamination procedures provided by the hospital, and on the selection and use of PPE (OSHA, 1992c). Training that is relevant to the required competencies counts toward the 8-hour requirement, even if the training is provided as a separate course. For example, training on PPE that will be used during victim decontamination activities may be applied towards the 8-hour minimum Operations Level training requirement, regardless of whether the PPE training is conducted as part of a specific HAZWOPER training course or as part of another training program (OSHA, 1992c).

First Responder Awareness Level training also counts towards the 8-hour requirement for Operations Level training. This point is clarified in a recent letter of interpretation issued by OSHA: "...if you spend two hours training employees in the required competencies for First Responder Awareness Level as described in 29 CFR 1910.120(q)(6)(i)(A)-(F), then you would need to spend at least six additional hours training employees in the required competencies for First Responder Operations Level as described in 29 CFR 1910.120(q) (6)(ii)(A)-(F). Depending on the employees' job duties and prior education and experience, more than eight hours of training may be needed" (OSHA, 2003).

As an alternative to the 8-hour training requirement, the HAZWOPER standard allows employees to demonstrate competence in specific areas, presented in 29 CFR 1910.120(q)(6)(ii) and reproduced in the section, Competencies for First Responder Operations Level Training at page 35. OSHA reaffirmed this point in a letter of interpretation, stating "...employees with sufficient experience may objectively demonstrate the required competencies instead of completing eight hours of training" (OSHA, 2003). However, it is important to note that in most hospital settings it might be difficult to ensure that employees have sufficient experience to waive the training requirement. Most hospital employees do not have extensive experience with hazardous materials or PAPRs, and decontamination activities are performed infrequently.

Hospitals must document how training requirements are met. This is particularly important whenev-

---

[41] State Plan States enforce standards, including the HAZWOPER standard and its training requirements, which are "at least as effective as" Federal OSHA's standards, and therefore may have more stringent or supplemental requirements.

[42] JCAHO standards require: (1) identification and assignment of personnel to cover all necessary staff positions under emergency conditions, (2) education as to their specific roles and responsibilities during emergencies, (3) information and skills required to perform assigned duties during emergencies, and (4) testing the response phase of EMPs twice a year, including a mandatory practice drill relevant to the priority emergencies in the organization's HVA.

er hospitals allow employees to satisfy any portion of the training requirement through other related training or through demonstration of competence. The HAZWOPER standard requires and an OSHA letter of interpretation confirms that "the employer must certify in writing the comparable training or demonstrated competencies" (OSHA, 2003).

Annual refresher training is specified under 1910.120(q)(8)(i), or the parallel State Plan standards; however, the length of the refresher training is not specified. Instead, the standard requires that employees trained at the First Responder Operations Level "shall receive annual refresher training of sufficient content and duration to maintain their competencies, or shall demonstrate competency in those areas at least yearly." Additionally, the hospital must document that refresher training was performed, or alternatively, keep a record of how the employee demonstrated competency.

The initial and annual refresher training to the HAZWOPER First Responder Operations Level must be provided to all hospital personnel who have been designated to provide treatment, triage, decontamination, or other services to contaminated individuals or who may reasonably be expected to come in contact with those individuals arriving at the hospital. Training core elements must include:

- Understanding the hospital emergency operations plan and their roles in the response.
- Site safety, including risks to receiving personnel.
- Appropriate selection and use of PPE.
- Decontamination procedures.

The Operations Level training related to the use of PPE must include topics such as those specified by OSHA's Personal Protective Equipment standard (29 CFR 1910.132). Under that standard, training must be provided to each employee who is required to use PPE. At a minimum, that training must cover the following:

- When PPE is necessary.
- What PPE is necessary.
- How to properly put on, remove, adjust, and wear PPE.
- Limitations of PPE.
- Proper care, maintenance, useful life, and disposal of PPE.

Employees must demonstrate their understanding of the training by showing they can use the PPE properly, prior to using the protective equipment in the workplace. Refresher training is warranted when the employee cannot demonstrate proficiency in the proper care and use of the PPE, when changes in the workplace render the previous training obsolete, or when changes in the type of PPE to be used render the previous training obsolete. OSHA specifies that the hospital must maintain a written record of employee PPE training.

Operations Level training also must include training required by OSHA's Respiratory Protection standard (29 CFR 1910.134), or the parallel State Plan standards. Specifically, any employee who must wear a respirator must be trained in the proper use and limitations of that device prior to its use in the workplace. The training must be comprehensive enough that the employee is able to demonstrate knowledge of the seven training topics specified in the standard and outlined below. The employee also must be able to demonstrate competence in wearing the complete PPE ensemble, including respirator, protective garment, gloves, boots, and other safety equipment required for the employee's role. Refresher training is required *at least annually*, or sooner if changes in the workplace or type of respirator render previous training inadequate. Refresher training is also required if the employee does not demonstrate proficiency in the proper care and use of the respirator, or any other time when retraining appears necessary to ensure safe respirator use.

At a minimum, training under OSHA's Respiratory Protection standard must cover the following topic areas:

- The nature of the respiratory hazard, and why a respirator is needed.
- Respirator capabilities, limitations, and consequences, if the respirator is not used correctly.
- How to handle respirator malfunctions and other emergencies.
- How to inspect, put on, remove, use, and check seals on the respirator.
- Maintenance and storage procedures.
- When to change cartridges on APRs.
- How to recognize medical signs and symptoms that may limit or prevent effective use of a respirator.
- General requirements of the respiratory protection program.

Note that first receivers who wear respiratory protection must be deemed medically qualified to do so, following the process required by 29 CFR 1910.134(e)(1) through (e)(6) of OSHA's Respiratory Protection standard. Employees who wear tight-fitting respirators also must be properly fit tested as required in 29 CFR 1910.134(f) (Respiratory Protection), or the parallel State Plan standards.

AWARENESS LEVEL TRAINING

First Responder Awareness Level training is required for those employees who work in the contaminant-free Hospital Post-decontamination Zone, but might be in a position to identify a contaminated victim who arrived unannounced. This group includes ED clinicians, ED clerks, and ED triage staff who would be responsible for notifying hospital authorities of the arrival, but would not reasonably be anticipated to have contact with the contaminated victims, their belongings, equipment, or waste. The group also includes decontamination system set-up crew members and patient tracking clerks, if their roles do not put them in contact with contaminated victims, their belongings, equipment, or waste (e.g., setting up the decontamination system before victims arrive, or tracking patients from a location outside of the decontamination zone).

First Responder Awareness Level training also is required for hospital security guards who work *away from* the Hospital Decontamination Zone, but who may be involved tangentially in a mass casualty event (specifically, those security personnel who would not reasonably be anticipated to come in contact with contaminated victims, their belongings, equipment, or waste) (OSHA 1991b). Security staff assigned to roles in the Hospital Decontamination Zone would require a higher level of training (e.g., First Responder Operations Level).

Training requirements for First Responder Awareness Level appear under 29 CFR 1910.120(q)(6)(i), which does not require a specific minimum training duration, but outlines topics to be covered (competencies the employee must acquire). As with Operations Level training, the HAZWOPER standard allows an alternative to the Awareness Level training requirement. Training can be waived if the employee has had sufficient experience to objectively demonstrate competency in specific areas. These areas are listed in 29 CFR 1910.120(q)(6)(i), or the parallel State Plan standards, and reproduced in the section First Responder Awareness Level Training at page 36.

Annual refresher training is required for employees trained at the Awareness Level. As with Operations Level refresher training, the class content must be adequate to maintain the employees' competence, and the hospital must document the training or the method used to demonstrate the employees' competence.

BRIEFING FOR SKILLED SUPPORT PERSONNEL WHOSE PARTICIPATION WAS NOT PREVIOUSLY ANTICIPATED

A member of the staff who has not been designated, but is unexpectedly called on to minister to a contaminated victim, or perform other work in the Hospital Decontamination Zone, is considered skilled support personnel. Examples include a medical specialist or a trade person, such as an electrician. These individuals must receive expedient orientation to site operations immediately prior to providing such services (OSHA, 1997). The orientation must include:

- Nature of the hazard (if known).
- Expected duties.
- Appropriate use of PPE.
- Other appropriate safety and health precautions (e.g., decontamination procedures).

As part of the briefing, these personnel also must be medically cleared for respirator use and properly fit tested (if wearing a tight-fitting respirator), as required by 29 CFR 1910.134 (Respiratory Protection), or the parallel State Plan standards. See the section Instruction for Employees Whose Participation in the Hospital Decontamination Zone Was Not Previously Anticipated at page 36 for additional information on briefing content.

While a just in time briefing during the response is the only *required* training for these personnel, time and resource limitations inherent in a crisis likely will diminish the effectiveness of such training. Thus, hospitals should diligently consider the broad range of skills/capabilities that may be required within the Decontamination Zone during a mass casualty event and attempt to identify and train all persons who may be called to work in the Decontamination Zone prior to a mass casualty event.

TRAINING SIMILAR TO THAT OUTLINED IN THE HAZARD COMMUNICATION STANDARD

Hospitals should consider offering a basic level of training for other employees in the ED, such as housekeeping staff. This group could include those personnel who do not have a role in the decontamination process, reasonably would not be expected to

encounter self-referred contaminated patients, and reasonably would not be expected to come in contact with contaminated victims, their belongings, equipment, or waste. OSHA's Hazard Communication standard offers a useful model for appropriate training, which could include general information on the hospital's emergency procedures and plans for mass casualty incidents involving contaminated victims, steps the employees can take to protect themselves (usually by leaving the area), and the measures the hospital has implemented to protect employees in the ED. While not required under the OSH Act, such training could help to ensure that all staff in the ED understand what precautions and actions would (and would not) be expected of them if an incident occurred.

SUMMARY OF TRAINING FOR FIRST RECEIVERS

Table 4 summarizes OSHA's current guidance on training first receivers for mass casualty emergencies. References to related OSHA interpretation letters are included. Employees are categorized according to zone (namely, *Hospital Decontamination Zone and Post-decontamination Zone*); whether they have designated roles in the zone; and the likelihood of contact with contaminated victims, their belongings, equipment, or waste. Hospitals should note that the training levels presented are *minimum* training levels and can be increased or augmented, as appropriate, to better protect employees, other patients, and the facility in general.

Table 4. Training for First Receivers

MANDATORY TRAINING	FIRST RECEIVERS COVERED	REFERENCE
First Responder OPERATIONS LEVEL[N] **Initial training** **Annual refresher** Both initial and refresher training may be satisfied by demonstration of competence.	*All employees with designated roles in the Hospital Decontamination Zone.[O] This group includes, but is not limited to:* • Decontamination staff, including decontamination victim inspectors; clinicians who will triage and/or stabilize victims prior to decontamination;[P] security staff [e.g., crowd control and controlling access to the emergency department (ED)]; set-up crew; and patient tracking clerks.	OSHA, 2003, 1992c, 1999
Briefing at the time of the incident[Q,R]	*Other employees whose role in the Hospital Decontamination Zone was not previously anticipated (i.e., who are called in incidentally). (e.g., a medical specialist or trade person, such as an electrician.)*	OSHA, 1997
First Responder AWARENESS LEVEL **Initial training** **Annual refresher** Both initial and refresher training may be satisfied by demonstration of competence.	*a) Security personnel, set-up crew, and patient tracking clerks assigned only to patient receiving areas proximate to the Decontamination Zone where they might encounter, but are <u>not</u> expected to have contact with, contaminated victims, their belongings, equipment, or waste.* *b) ED clinicians, clerks, triage staff, and other employees associated with emergency departments, who might encounter self-referred contaminated victims (and their belongings, equipment, or waste) without receiving prior notification that such victims have been contaminated.*	OSHA, 1991a, 1991b

RECOMMENDED TRAINING	PERSONNEL COVERED	REFERENCE
Training similar to that outlined in the Hazard Communication standard[S]	*Other personnel in the Hospital Post-decontamination Zone who reasonably would not be expected to encounter or come in contact with unannounced contaminated victims, their belongings, equipment, or waste.[T,U]* *(e.g., other ED staff, such as housekeepers.)*	29 CFR 1910.1200(h)

[N] The employer must certify that personnel trained at the "First Responder Operations Level" have received at least eight hours of specific training (which can include Awareness Level training, PPE training, and training exercise/drills), or have had sufficient experience to objectively demonstrate competency in specific key areas. Refresher training must be provided annually and must be of sufficient content and duration to maintain competencies. Alternatively, the employee may demonstrate competence (i.e., skills) (OSHA HAZWOPER 29 CFR 1910.120(q)(6)(ii)). Participation in training exercises/drills is recommended to ensure competency during initial and refresher training.

[O] The *Hospital Decontamination Zone* includes any areas where the type and quantity of hazardous substance is unknown and where contaminated victims, contaminated equipment, or contaminated waste may be present. It is reasonably anticipated that employees in this zone might have exposure to contaminated victims, their belongings, equipment, or waste. This zone includes, but is not limited to: places where initial triage and/or medical stabilization of possibly contaminated victims occur, pre-decontamination waiting (staging) areas for victims, the actual decontamination area, and the post-decontamination victim inspection area. This area will typically end at the ED door.

[P] The term *clinician* includes physicians, nurses, nurse practitioners, physicians' assistants, and others.

[Q] The briefing must include (at a minimum) instruction on wearing the appropriate PPE, the nature of the hazard, expected duties, and the safety and health precautions the individual should take (OSHA, 1997 (Whittaker); 29 CFR 1910.120(q)(4)).

[R] Note that the individual must be medically qualified (29 CFR 1910.134), fitted (1910.132 and .134), and trained (1910.132 and .134) to use the required PPE. These qualifications are difficult to achieve at the time of the incident and, whenever possible, should be accomplished prior to an incident.

[S] While HAZCOM training is not required pursuant to the OSH Act for most of the scenarios contemplated in this document, a prudent employer may consider adopting and appropriately modifying the training provisions in the HAZCOM standard to provide information to personnel who would not be expected to come in contact with unannounced contaminated victims, their belongings, equipment, or waste.

[T] The *Hospital Post-decontamination Zone* is an area considered uncontaminated. Equipment and personnel are not expected to become contaminated in this area. At a hospital receiving contaminated victims, the Hospital Post-decontamination Zone includes the ED (unless contaminated).

[U] If the ED becomes contaminated, the hospital's decontamination procedures must be activated by the properly trained and equipped employees (refer to the Hospital Decontamination Zone in this table and Table 3).

The following appendices provide references and examples which might be useful to hospitals developing or upgrading emergency management plans (EMPs). OSHA offers these examples for informational purposes only and does not recommend one option over the many effective alternatives that exist.

This Appendix supplements the *Best Practices from OSHA* by providing useful background information on how various aspects of a hospital's preparation, response, and recovery impact employee protection during hazardous substance emergencies. Look in Appendix A for:

PREPAREDNESS

The following discussion provides examples of ways hospitals have attempted to enhance employee protection as part of general preparedness for mass casualty emergencies involving contaminated victims. This discussion is designed to further worker health and safety by referencing practices and procedures considered and/or adopted in the healthcare community. However, statements in this appendix cannot create nor diminish obligations under the Occupational Safety and Health (OSH) Act.

In making preparations, hospitals must consider key assumptions regarding communication, resources, and victims. When developing plans, hospitals should anticipate:

- Victims will arrive with little or no warning to the hospital.
- Information regarding the hazardous agent(s) will not be available immediately.
- A large number of victims will be self-referred victims (as much as 80 percent of the total number of victims).
- Victims will not necessarily have been decontaminated prior to arriving at the hospital.
- A high percentage of people arriving at the hospital will have experienced little or no exposure and this eventuality should be considered in decontamination plans.
- Most victims will go to the hospital closest to the site where the emergency occurred.
- Victims will use other entrances in addition to the emergency department (ED).

Sources: Auf der Heide, 2002; Barbera and Macintyre, 2003; Vogt, 2002; Okumura et al., 1996.

Administrators making preparations for mass casualty incidents should note that hospitals are part of the community's critical infrastructure and continuity of operations must be maintained.

CUSTOMIZING HOSPITAL EMERGENCY MANAGEMENT PLANS

The hospital emergency management plan (EMP) outlines how the facility will respond to an emergency. The plan should address the hazards the hospital will encounter, identify the hospital's role in the response, and serve as a road map for incident preparation, response, and recovery.

No organization can prepare fully for every conceivable emergency. To use resources effectively, a hospital requires information that will help emergency planners make informed decisions about the type, probability, severity, and impact of specific hazards to which the hospital might be subject. A hazard vulnerability analysis (HVA) assists a hospital in organizing this information, which is used to customize the hazard assessment for personal protective equipment (PPE) selection (a critical aspect of the EMP). The Joint Committee for Accreditation of Healthcare Organizations (JCAHO) requires an HVA as the first step in emergency planning (JCAHO, 2004). Specific information on conducting HVAs may be obtained directly from JCAHO.

The HVA and resulting preparations are only as specific to the individual hospital as the information on which preparation decisions are based. Important modifying factors include the hospital's role in the community, how up-to-date the hospital's EMP is, and formal planning agreements between the hospital and other organizations that have roles in emergency response activities. With knowledge of these details, hospitals can customize EMPs and effectively tailor preparedness (including employee protection) to address the circumstances relevant to that hospital.

Using Information from a Hazard Vulnerability Analysis

As noted previously, an HVA helps hospitals organize information and guide decision-making. A thorough HVA can serve as the basis for informed decisions regarding the training and equipment employees will require to protect themselves under foreseeable emergency scenarios.

The hospitals interviewed use variations of a few publicly available HVA formats. See Appendix F for examples of two formats (additional examples are available from other sources). The tool is often slightly modified by the individual hospital to include additional information that the hospital finds helpful for making decisions or communicating with management.

A popular HVA, an electronic spreadsheet, prompts the user to enter a numerical rating (e.g., 1 to 3) for various factors associated with each of numerous listed threats (both from a standard list and additional hazards added by the user). JCAHO (2002) offers a

matrix of threats that hospitals might consider. The user generates (or the spreadsheet calculates) a hazard vulnerability score based on the inputs. The inputs may be weighted to reflect the importance of certain information to the final score. Hospitals use both the final score and the individual numerical rating inputs to identify and rank priority areas that should receive administrative attention or resources.

Other hospitals use a tabular format HVA and more descriptive text input to guide the user through the analysis. The tables can provide more information, but are also more cumbersome for evaluating a large selection of threats. Because these formats are more likely to have been developed in-house, they tend to be more diverse.

None of the HVA formats have been validated to determine whether the inputs and final assessment accurately reflect hazard vulnerability. Nevertheless, an informal qualitative review conducted by the developer of one HVA spreadsheet tool suggested that independent users, when operating in similar hospital and community environments, do generally arrive at similar conclusions regarding vulnerability and priorities for improvement (Saruwatari, 2003).

The hospitals interviewed for this project agree that the HVA should be updated frequently and reviewed at least annually, as required by JCAHO (2004). By collaborating with Local Emergency Planning Committees (LEPCs), hospitals can keep current with information on changes in threats in their localities.[43] Hospital D noted that, if appropriate, resources could be reallocated sooner if emergency managers are able to update the HVA as new information arrives (e.g., emerging threats), rather than waiting for an annual review cycle.[44] These changes can also modify the local hospital's vulnerability to those hazards. As an example, Hospital D had rated "preparation for chlorine-related emergencies" as a top priority. When the local potable water facility changed processes, the threat of a large-scale chlorine emergency was eliminated from the community. Upon revising the HVA, Hospital D was able to redirect resources to address the next most urgent threat without waiting until the next annual review cycle.

Characteristics of the community (e.g., businesses, chemical inventory, population, transportation lines,

clandestine drug labs, and possible targets of terrorism) influence the type of hazardous substance-related emergencies that a hospital might reasonably anticipate. This information should be considered in the HVA. These factors range from the number and condition of victims that the hospital might rreasonably anticipate, to the rate at which hazard information could become available during an emergency.

Identifying the Hospital's Role in the Community

The community in which a hospital is located and the hospital's role in that community impact emergency preparations on several levels. Hospital D's emergency manager suggested that the real objective of emergency planning is "community preparedness, and a hospital's preparedness represents only one component." For the purposes of this discussion, "community" is defined as the local population center that the hospital serves on a day-to-day basis, as well as any additional population centers from which the hospital would reasonably expect to receive victims in the event of a mass casualty emergency involving hazardous substances.

Fully coordinated planning helps hospitals identify their roles in their communities. Roles vary considerably with individual circumstances, but ultimately have a strong impact on the conditions and hazards for which a hospital must plan employee protection. Examples of roles some hospitals fill (or expect to fill) in their communities include:

- Providing decontamination and treatment for any and all victims.
- Promoting a wider level of preparedness in the community by providing low-cost hazard communication or hazardous waste operations and emergency response (HAZWOPER) training for local government and business emergency response personnel.
- Providing information and services related to emergency preparedness (e.g., respirator medical clearance).
- Participating actively in multi-disciplined community-based planning and preparedness activities, such as LEPCs (e.g., Hospital D reports devoting a minimum of 12 man-hours per week to its active role in community preparedness. This time is in addition to the hours spent managing the hospital's internal preparations).

The hospitals interviewed for this project also note that, in addition to a better coordinated community

[43] Visit www.epa.gov/swercepp/lepclist.htm to see listings for LEPCs by location.

[44] See acknowledgments at the beginning of this document for a brief statement about the hospitals interviewed for this guidance.

emergency response plan, they receive additional financial, informational, and business benefits from active participation in community-focused emergency preparedness and planning. The following list indicates benefits that hospitals can derive from an active role in community emergency preparedness:

- Increased access to community records, which help managers improve the accuracy of the HVA and help the hospital customize its EMP.[45]
- Increased access to grants and other financial resources.
- Group buying power that allows for volume discounts or government rates (including reduced sales tax) for equipment and supplies.
- More opportunities to contain costs by sharing or trading expertise, training resources, equipment, and services.
- Greater opportunity to tailor community drills so they test the hospital's emergency plans.
- Increased opportunities to network and develop useful alliances with emergency first responders and other emergency planners (particularly useful for resolving complex issues that emerge as groups coordinate their activities under difficult circumstances).
- Greater visibility in the community and increased respect as a valued resource and partner (including among business leaders).

Updating Emergency Management Plans

EMPs should be reviewed periodically for the same reasons the HVA is updated — situations change.[46] Common changes that can impact employee protection include the types of foreseeable hazardous situations that might be encountered in an emergency, the anticipated needs of the community, the availability of other emergency response organizations to fill certain

roles, the type of equipment available to protect employees, and personnel turnover.

Hospitals should already be in compliance with applicable OSHA health and safety standards, such as those listed below (or parallel OSHA-approved State Plan standards). Additionally, during the periodic EMP evaluation, hospitals should review the regulations to ensure the plan continues to be compliant.

- OSH Act – General Duty Clause (Section (5)(a)(1))
- HAZWOPER – 29 CFR 1910.120(q).
- Personal Protective Equipment – 29 CFR 1910.132.
- Eye and Face Protection – 29 CFR 1910.133.
- Respiratory Protection – 29 CFR 1910.134.[47]
- Hand Protection – 29 CFR 1910.138.
- Hazard Communication – 29 CFR 1910.1200(h).
- Bloodborne Pathogens – 29 CFR 1910.1030.
- Ethylene Oxide – 29 CFR 1910.1047.
- Formaldehyde – 29 CFR 1910.1048.

Coordinating Emergency Plans with Other Organizations

Well-coordinated EMPs ensure that hospitals are aware of the capabilities of first responders and other hospitals, as well as what the local professional and response community expects from them.[48] Coordinated plans encourage open lines of communication and improve the safety of both victims and healthcare workers. The following example demonstrates the value of coordinated EMPs. After problems were identified during a drill, Hospital D determined that healthcare workers needed faster access to information from hazardous materials incident sites. Initially, the fire department felt that Hospital D's request for more timely information would be too burdensome during life-threatening emergencies. When the two organizations met, however, they each learned the reasons behind the other's needs. As a result, the first responders recognized that, by coordinating efforts, they could enhance the first receivers' ability to provide rapid and appropriate care to victims. The fire department was able to modify its own EMP to incorporate direct communication between the hospital and a representative of the incident commander at the scene.

---

[45] Hospitals report that some useful community records include statistics on local hazardous materials incidents, population census and demographic information, local probability rates for natural disasters, Chamber of Commerce data, and information on types and quantities of hazardous substances used by local industry (e.g., EPA Emergency Planning and Community Right-to-Know Act (EPCRA) Section 311/312, 40 CFR Part 370, Hazardous chemical storage reporting requirements, described in further detail at: http://yosemite.epa.gov/oswer/ceppoweb.nsf/vwResourcesByFilename/epcra.pdf/$File/epcra.pdf.)

[46] JCAHO (2004) requires that both the HVA and the EMP be evaluated annually, with particular attention to "its objectives, scope, functionality and effectiveness."

[47] For additional information on the OSHA Respiratory Protection standard, see http://www.osha.gov/SLTC/etools/respiratory/index.html.

[48] JCAHO (2004) requires, and OSHA (2001) recommends, that organizations coordinate emergency management planning efforts.

The hospitals interviewed for this project mentioned several methods by which they improve EMP coordination and communication:

- Use an incident command system compatible with the National Incident Management System (NIMS) structure.[49,50]
- Get to know members of the other organizations and the details of their plans. Seek opportunities to improve communication.
- Seek input from other organizations (such as local emergency planning groups) when developing or updating plans.
- Use compatible forms of communication, such as radios capable of operating on the same frequency. Keep compatibility in mind when purchasing equipment.
- Participate in multi-organizational drills. Execute multi-organizational drills that test the way organizations interact under adverse conditions.
- Analyze drills to identify areas that need improvement and meet directly with the other organizations to develop action plans that provide mutually agreeable, practical solutions to problems. Bear in mind that a solution suggested by one party might not be feasible for another organization to implement.
- Test inter-organizational communication systems at every opportunity (e.g., fire department, law enforcement, emergency medical services, environmental management, and other hospitals).[51]

Barbera and Macintyre (2003) suggest the following organizations with which hospitals should coordinate:

- Public health groups (including special laboratories).
- Local emergency management organizations (e.g., LEPCs).
- Emergency medical services.
- Law enforcement, at all levels.

PREPARING STAFF AND MANAGEMENT

Applicable Standards

Organizations, such as OSHA, those states operating OSHA-approved State Plans, JCAHO, the National Fire Protection Association (NFPA), and other state or local government agencies, set standards that govern employee preparation, particularly regarding employee training and medical evaluations. OSHA standards, or the parallel State Plan standards, relevant to the training of first receivers include the HAZWOPER, Personal Protective Equipment, Respiratory Protection, and Hazard Communication standards.[52] Hospitals with decontamination facilities should also comply with the requirement for medical evaluations contained in the HAZWOPER and Respiratory Protection standards.

JCAHO (2004) requires "an orientation and education program for all personnel, including licensed independent practitioners, who participate in implementing the emergency management plan." When plans involve management of chemical hazards, OSHA's HAZWOPER and hazard communication (HAZCOM) standards complement the JCAHO requirements by providing specific topics that should be addressed during the training. Other requirements of these standards might also apply (e.g., training duration, demonstration of skills, and retraining), depending on whether the HAZWOPER (Hospital Decontamination Zone) or the HAZCOM (Hospital Post-decontamination Zone) standard is in effect. NFPA (2002) suggests competencies for incident commanders and others responding to hazardous materials incidents.

---

[49] An example of a NIMS-compatible system, the publicly available Hospital Emergency Incident Command System (HEICS), uses the same structure and vocabulary as the widely used Fire Department Incident Command System. Emergency services leaders report that the respective command systems interface well, without loss of organizational identity (San Mateo County HSA, 1998). A brief introduction to HEICS appears in Appendix G.

[50] For additional information on incident command systems see http://www.osha.gov/SLTC/etools/ics/index.html and http://www.emsa.ca.gov/Dms2/HISTORY.HTM (also attached to this guidance document as Appendix G).

[51] JCAHO standards require cooperative planning among healthcare organizations that together provide services to a contiguous geographic area (for example, among hospitals serving a town or borough). Such planning is intended to facilitate the timely sharing of information about: (1) essential elements of their command structures and control centers for emergency response; (2) names, roles, and telephone numbers of individuals in their commands structures; (3) resources and assets that could potentially be shared or pooled in an emergency response; and (4) names of patients and deceased individuals brought to their organizations to facilitate identification and location of victims of the emergency.

---

[52] HAZWOPER – 29 CFR 1910.120(q); Personal Protective Equipment – 29 CFR 1910.132; Respiratory Protection – 29 CFR 1910.134; Hazard Communication – 29 CFR 1910.1200(h).

[53] Employer obligations pursuant to the HAZWOPER and HAZCOM standards are determined by the hazards to which it is reasonably possible for employees to be exposed, given the nature and locations of the employees' work.

Maintaining Decontamination Teams

A challenge for any hospital is the need to maintain a decontamination team, without compromising the ability of hospital departments to provide medical treatment for patients.

Hospitals interviewed for this project use employees from a range of specialties to maintain minimal staffing levels in patient care areas. In addition to drawing limited staff from the ED, Hospital A suggests including individuals from departments such as mental health, facilities and engineering, and security on decontamination teams.

The hospitals also indicate that it is often possible to identify individuals in unrelated departments who are uniquely qualified to serve on the team due to previous military experience, work history, or volunteer service. Hospital A staffs a particularly large decontamination team (over 100 members) by drawing from employees with relevant skills from past experience in fire departments, emergency medical services, rescue units, HAZMAT or hazardous waste handling, National Guard, and military reserve units. In these cases, the previous experience might be a more important selection criterion than the individual's day-to-day role in the hospital. Hospital A avoids assigning unwilling staff to their team, citing the advantages of volunteer team members' enthusiasm and willingness to participate in training and drills.

Decontamination teams might include individuals who perform the following functions:

- *Decontamination team leader – responsible for management of the decontamination operation.[54]
- *Decontamination safety officer – responsible for monitoring the decontamination area for developing hazards and for ensuring team safety.
- *Pre-decontamination triage – responsible for assessing medical status and prioritizing victims for decontamination.
- Decontamination system set-up.
- Security.
- Decontamination hospital attendants.
- Post-decontamination inspection.
- Cleanup and decontamination crew (surfaces, equipment, human and hazardous wastes).

- Other roles that might be performed in the Hospital Decontamination Zone under some circumstances (e.g., patient tracking, assistants helping team members with PPE).

The size of the decontamination team depends on the minimum number of people required to operate the decontamination system and implement the hospital's decontamination procedures. Activities involving a few victims and small decontamination systems usually require only a few staff members, each of whom might fill several functional roles. Hick et al. (2003b) suggest that a small hospital might have a 2-person team available at all times, while a metropolitan hospital might need a 5-person team available to work in the Hospital Decontamination Zone, with additional personnel on-call to allow for staff rotation. According to Hick, the 5-person team would include one person handling triage and coordinating pre-decontamination treatment, two people working with non-ambulatory victims, and two team members working with ambulatory victims. During a major emergency in a metropolitan area, hospitals might be required to continue operations "at maximum capacity for at least 2 to 4 hours, with appropriate staff rotations" (Hick et al., 2003b).

Another hospital organization advocates a 12-member (minimum) decontamination team, all wearing PPE. Although it is recognized that smaller hospitals would not be able to staff such a robust team, the rationale may illustrate useful points. Under this model, the Northern Virginia Hospital Alliance calls for a single "team leader," three team members responsible for conducting ambulatory decontamination (one to assist in the undressing, one to supervise showering, and one to assist in the re-dressing), four team members to participate in the care of non-ambulatory patients, and four security personnel to preserve the perimeter of the Hospital Decontamination Zone.

Orienting and Training Personnel

First receiver training that was discussed previously in the Personal Protective Equipment section is summarized here:

First Responder Operations Level training is required for employees (including security staff) who have a role in the Hospital Decontamination Zone, as well as the hospital's contamination cleanup crew.[55]

---

[54] Hick et al. (2003b) recommend job action sheets be developed for these positions and other decontamination team members who serve key roles. Sample job action sheets are available at www.hazmatforhealthcare.org.

[55] First Responder Operations Level and Awareness Level training requirements appear in OSHA's HAZWOPER standard, 29 CFR 1910.120(q), (or parallel State Plan standards).

OSHA
Occupational Safety and
Health Administration

First Responder Awareness Level training is required for ED clerks and ED triage staff who might identify unannounced contaminated victims (then notify the proper authority) and security staff working outside the Hospital Decontamination Zone.

A briefing at the time of the incident is required for employees whose roles in the Hospital Decontamination Zone could not be anticipated before the incident ("skilled support personnel" – e.g., a medical specialist or a trade person, such as an electrician).

Information similar to hazard communication training is recommended for ED staff and other employees who work in the ED (Hospital Post-decontamination Zone), provided contaminated victims would not have access to them.

Competencies for First Responder Operations Level Training

The HAZWOPER standard, paragraph 1910.120(q)(6)(ii) requires that employees trained at the First Responder Operations Level shall have received at least eight hours of training or have had sufficient experience to objectively demonstrate competency (e.g., in exercises and drills) in the following areas:

- *An understanding of what hazardous substances are, and the risks associated with them in an incident.[56]
- *An understanding of the potential outcomes associated with an emergency when hazardous substances are present.
- *The ability to recognize the presence of hazardous substances in an emergency through signs and symptoms of exposure.
- *The ability to identify the hazardous substances, if possible.
- *An understanding of their role in the hospital's emergency response plan, including site security and control, and decontamination procedures (OSHA, 1992c).
- *The ability to realize the need for additional resources and to make appropriate notifications to the communication center.
- Knowledge of the basic hazard and risk assessment techniques.
- Know how to select and use proper PPE.

- An understanding of basic hazardous materials terms.
- Know how to perform basic control, containment, and/or confinement operations within the capabilities of the resources and PPE available.
- Know how to implement basic decontamination procedures.
- An understanding of the relevant standard operating procedures and termination procedures.

Several examples of HAZWOPER First Responder Operations Level training curricula are available for hospitals preparing employees to conduct decontamination activities (HAZMAT for Healthcare, 2003; CA EMSA, 2003a; VA, 2003; Sutter Health, 2002). However, these curricula are not necessarily designed as 8-hour presentations (some are longer, others are shorter and intended for use when employees are able to demonstrate specific areas of competency).

Hospital A and Hospital G opt to provide more than 8 hours of training to decontamination team employees. Hospital A requires staff who will have a direct role in decontamination activities to undergo 24 hours of initial training and an additional 16 hours of refresher training annually. Employees can satisfy some of the training requirement by attending monthly educational team meetings. Other training is provided using a standard course curriculum developed by the Department of Veterans Affairs.[57]

Hospital G is in the process of changing from a single yearly 8-hour course curriculum to a program that provides twelve 1-hour sessions. The emergency planner believes that an annual training day is not the best condition for learning and skills retention. Under the new system, Hospital G divides the required training topics into 12 modules, one for each month, including several opportunities to don PPE over the course of a year. The monthly module will be presented several times on each shift. Although the net hours of training per student will be greater annually, the departments might find it less burdensome to release students for the shorter classes. Thus, instructors will teach fewer classes, resulting in a net savings in man-hours.

---

[56] * Indicates the item is also a competency for Awareness Level training.

[57] Hospital A feels this level of training is the minimum required to maintain its world-class decontamination team, which drills with out-of-state military units and, due to location, would be called upon to decontaminate victims from a national chemical weapons arsenal, should an accident occur.

As mentioned earlier, 8 hours of First Responder Operations Level training might not be necessary for employees who have sufficient experience. These employees are allowed to demonstrate competency as an alternative to 8 hours of training. In most hospital settings, however, it might be difficult to ensure that employees have sufficient experience to waive the training requirement. Most hospital employees do not have extensive experience with hazardous materials and decontamination activities are performed infrequently, thus more than 8 hours of training may be helpful to ensure competence. Employees particularly benefit from the practical experience they gain during training provided as part of exercises and drills. These events also offer employees an opportunity to demonstrate competence in critical areas.

Competencies for First Responder Awareness Level Training

First responders at the awareness level shall have sufficient training or have had sufficient experience to objectively demonstrate competency in the following areas, as required by the HAZWOPER standard, paragraph 1910.120(q)(6)(i), (or the parallel State Plan standards):

- An understanding of what hazardous substances are, and the risks associated with them in an incident.
- An understanding of the potential outcomes associated with an emergency created when hazardous substances are present.
- The ability to recognize the presence of hazardous substances in an emergency.[58]
- The ability to identify the hazardous substances, if possible.
- An understanding of their role in the hospital's emergency response plan, including site security and control, and decontamination procedures (OSHA, 1992c).
- The ability to realize the need for additional resources and to make appropriate notifications to the communication center.

In addition to the HAZWOPER training topics, staff who might identify contaminated victims that arrive unannounced require specific instructions for handling the situation. Once ED clerks or staff suspect a patient is contaminated, they should be well trained in the following procedure:

1) Avoid physical contact with the patient.

2) Immediately notify supervisor and safety officer of possible hospital contamination.

3) Allow other properly trained and equipped staff to isolate and decontaminate the victim according to EMP.

All the hospitals interviewed for this project provide Awareness Level training for staff who have a role during decontamination activities, but are not directly involved in patient decontamination. As with First Responder Operations Level training, there is considerable variability in the extent of training provided at the Awareness Level. The hospitals use curricula that range from 2 to 4 hours and most require an annual refresher course of 1 to 4 hours.

Instruction for Employees Whose Participation in the Hospital Decontamination Zone Was Not Previously Anticipated

These personnel shall be given an initial briefing at the site prior to their participation in any emergency response. As specified in the HAZWOPER standard, paragraph 1910.120(q)(4), the initial briefing shall include instruction in the wearing of appropriate PPE, what chemical hazards are involved, and what duties are to be performed. All other appropriate safety and health precautions (e.g., PPE) provided to personnel in the Hospital Decontamination Zone shall be used to assure the safety and health of these personnel.

Training Similar to That Outlined in the Hazard Communication Standard

OSHA recommends some form of basic training for employees who work in the Hospital Post-decontamination Zone and who would not be expected to come in contact with unannounced contaminated victims, their belongings, equipment, or waste. This training could take a format similar to hazard communication which might include at least the following:

- Methods and observations that may be used to detect the presence of a hazardous substance in the work area (e.g., an odor or announcement by staff trained to identify possible contamination).
- General information on victims as a possible source of hazardous substances.
- The measures employees can take to protect themselves during an incident, including specific procedures the hospital has implemented to protect employees from exposure to hazardous sub-

---

[58] For first receivers, recognition of signs and symptoms would satisfy this training topic.

stances (e.g., emergency procedures for leaving the area). In developing a training program of this type, hospitals should consider which specific topics would best help this group of employees respond appropriately during an incident.

Monitoring Performance During Drills

All hospitals interviewed for this project conduct several types of drills. The hospitals note that the greatest value occurs when their EMPs are tested rigorously as part of the drill, when realistic scenarios are involved (including interaction with outside organizations), and when the hospital follows the drill with a detailed evaluation and post-drill action plan for improvement.

It is essential to the success of the EMP that drills are conducted and that they reflect the actual conditions, resources, and personnel that would be available during a real incident.

In addition to self-assessments, some hospitals find it helpful to receive a performance evaluation from an outside organization. Hospital C participated in a community-wide drill that was observed by a contractor hired specifically for that purpose. The hospital used the contractor's observations and comments to help prioritize the emergency management team's activities. Alternatively, organizations that share post-drill analysis can critique each other.[59] Any of these methods of assessment can lead to corrective actions and improved response, particularly if the process is formalized with hospital administrators.

Managing Internal Communications

The hospitals interviewed for this project report that they use a combination of methods for communicating with employees during an incident. As new information becomes available hospitals use any combination of the following methods to pass information to those who need it:

- Overhead public broadcasting systems[60]
- Telephones
- Cell phones
- Pagers
- Fax
- Runners with verbal or written messages
- Two-way radios
- E-mail and Intranet services

Overhead broadcasting systems, Intranet, and two-way radios are independent of external systems (such as telephone service) that might be impacted by a widespread emergency. A good EMP should consider the need for backup communications in the event of a power failure.

Principles of Risk Communication

Special care might be required in training healthcare workers regarding chemical, biological, or radiological hazards, particularly when the threat could be related to terrorism. Lundgren and McMakin (1998) recommend conducting an audience analysis to assess factors that will impact how information might best be presented. Non-clinical workers want basic information on the hazards, presented by a credible source with a clear message, and preferably in "detailed, role-specific training sessions that are ultimately tested by drills" (Thorne et al., 2003). To demonstrate training effectiveness, trainers should evaluate knowledge and skills by using objective measures such as pre- and post-training evaluations, as well as by observing performance.[61]

Information Dissemination During an Incident

Hospitals need to work with local emergency service organizations to provide clear, accurate information during large-scale emergencies. To avoid disseminating conflicting information, hospitals that use a National Incident Management System (NIMS)-compatible incident command system, such as HEICS, provide for an individual who will coordinate with other response groups and communicate with the media and other outside organizations.[62] A representative of the public affairs department often assumes this role.

---

[59] Other sources of critical observers might include peers from other hospitals, regulators, and members of fire department hazardous materials response teams.

[60] Overhead public broadcasting systems are used to report information directly or announce codes. One code indicates that designated staff should report to a meeting point to obtain information.

[61] JCAHO standards require an orientation and education program for all personnel who participate in implementing the EMP. This education addresses: (1) specific roles and responsibilities during emergencies, (2) methods used to recognize specific types of emergencies, and (3) information and skills required to perform assigned duties during emergencies.

[62] The Hospital Emergency Incident Command.

Monitoring Employee Health

Prior to an Incident

Hospitals A through G all indicate that they typically conduct a thorough baseline evaluation of an employee's health at the time the person is hired. Based on hospital policy, the employee's job category, or the hazards associated with tasks the employee performs, additional periodic health monitoring might also be provided.[63] Most of the hospitals interviewed for this project indicate that they have no special additional requirements for members of the decontamination team, unless the individual might wear a respirator. In that case, the employee receives a baseline evaluation and any follow-up evaluations needed to obtain the necessary medical clearance, as discussed below.

One of the hospitals interviewed follows a somewhat more rigorous medical monitoring program. Under this program, each member assigned to the decontamination team receives a periodic physical exam (often every 1 or 2 years), which includes a basic health screening. Evaluations for medical clearance to wear a respirator are incorporated into these exams.

The HAZWOPER standard requires that employees be provided periodic medical evaluations (annual or bi-annual) if they exhibit signs or symptoms of exposure, or if it is anticipated that the employee would be exposed to hazardous substances, in excess of the established permissible exposure limit (PEL), for 30 days per year or more.[64] Drills and practice sessions that do not involve hazardous substances would not count toward the 30 days.

The hospitals interviewed for this project also mentioned that prophylactic vaccinations and antidotes should be stockpiled for employees in case the need arises.

Medical Clearance for Respirator Use

The OSHA Respiratory Protection standard, in 29 CFR 1910.134(e), or the parallel State Plan standards, require employers to obtain, in writing, a medical opinion regarding an employee's ability to wear a respirator. The regulatory requirement applies regardless of whether other medical evaluations are needed under the HAZWOPER standard. It also applies to all types of respirators (including hooded powered air-purifying respirators [PAPRs]), with the exception of filtering facepiece respirators ("dust masks") used by employees on a voluntary basis (i.e., when the employer has determined that a health risk does not exist, but the employee nevertheless wishes to wear a respirator). An additional medical evaluation is required by paragraph 1910.134(e)(7) under certain circumstances. For example, an employee's ability to safely wear a respirator must be reevaluated when an increase in the employee's physical activities or the weight of the protective clothing would place an added burden on the employee.

During a Response

The combination of first receivers' activities and PPE often create a greater physical workload for employees than they experience during their normal daily jobs. Thermal stress (heat and cold stress) also impacts the period for which first receivers can perform their duties. Some hospitals monitor employee vital signs as one method of tracking employee response to these stressors. For example, Hospital A evaluates each employee's vital signs before that individual dons PPE. Prior to a team member donning a protective suit and hooded PAPR respirator, a technician records the individual's weight, vital signs, and recent medical history. This information is obtained as other team members assist the individual into the protective gear. If vital signs exceed predetermined limits set by the hospital organization, the individual is prohibited from wearing PPE that day and the team member's activities are restricted accordingly.

Decontamination safety officers at Hospital A report that during every drill conducted, they have rejected at least one participant (out of a dozen or more) due to elevated vital signs. When PPE is removed, vital signs and weight are recorded again. The employee's time in PPE is also recorded and tracked. Decontamination team members at Hospital A are generally permitted to wear a protective suit and hooded PAPR for 30 minutes at any one time, although this period can be adjusted up or down depending on workload, weather, and the condition of the first receiver. Appendices H and I provide examples of medical monitoring procedures and a separate vital signs checklist.

---

[63] All health monitoring results should be provided to the employee in a timely manner and in accordance with 29 CFR 1910.1020 (OSHA's standard on Access to Employee Exposure and Medical Records).

[64] Under most circumstances, first receivers would not be expected to perform decontamination duties in the presence of hazardous chemicals 30 days per year.

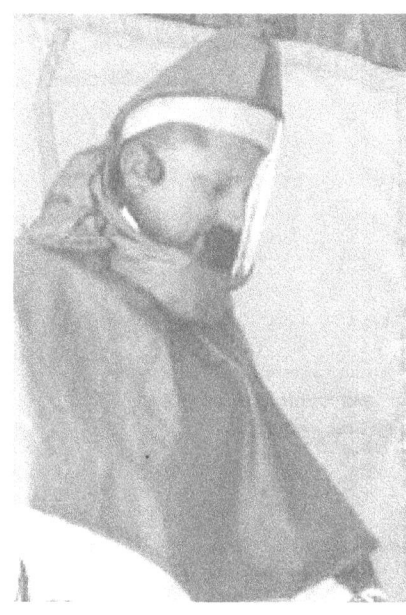

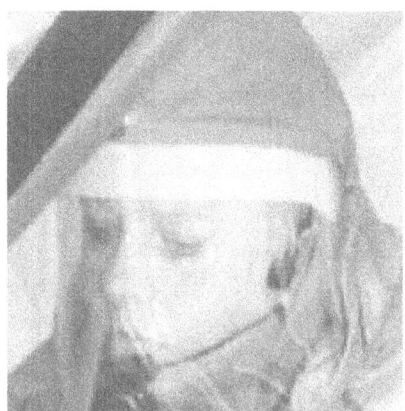

"Temple-transducer" style two-way radio headset stays in place under PAPR hoods.

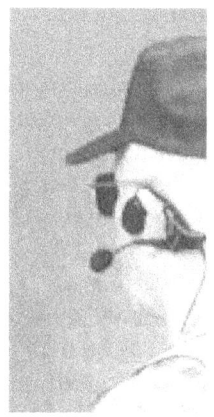

Detail of "temple-transducer" style radio headset.

Hospital A uses two-way headset radios to communicate with and monitor the health status of individuals who are wearing hooded PAPRs and protective suits in hot weather. This hospital found that a behind-the-head "temple transducer" style headset is more practical under PAPR hoods than "over-the-head" models, which tend to dislodge and are difficult to reposition without removing the hood.

Thermal Stress

Both heat and cold stress can decrease first responders' ability to work safely for extended periods. Hospital A believes that in its hot, humid southern climate, heat stress presents the greatest threat to employee health. To combat this hazard, the hospital uses a combination of administrative controls and cooling devices. As noted above, team members whose vital signs are outside prescribed starting parameters are not allowed to don respiratory protection.[65] To further reduce the risk of heat stress, the team makes extensive use of icepack vests.[66] Freezers for icepacks are located in the Safety Office, fire department, and elsewhere for easy access. Although

Hospital A recognizes that use of icepacks to combat heat stress is somewhat controversial, this hospital reports no problems among the many team members who have drilled over the years. Additionally, team members report that they find the icepack vests to be a comfortable asset in hot weather.

The American Conference of Governmental Industrial Hygienists (ACGIH) offers guidance for managing heat stress in employees wearing heavy protective clothing (ACGIH, 2001). This conservative approach uses a combination of common sense administrative controls (e.g., good hydration) and physiological measures of heat strain (remove worker if body core temperature exceeds 100.4 degrees Fahrenheit or heart rate exceeds 180 beats per minute (bpm) minus the employee's age, or is greater than 110 bpm one minute after peak exertion). Appendix I provides examples of vital sign monitoring schemes used by other groups.

Following an Incident

Incidents involving hazardous substances are typically one-time incidents and medical monitoring is not required unless an employee develops signs or symptoms related to an exposure. Following such an occurrence, the hospital's occupational health provider should follow the hospital's regular policy regarding a chemically exposed worker. If an employee becomes ill or develops signs or symptoms specifically suggesting exposure to a particular contaminant, Hospital A would follow a policy designed for first responders

---

[65] Vital signs may not exceed the following limits: diastolic blood pressure greater than 90 millimeters of mercury (mmHg), heart rate greater than 100 beats per minute, respiration greater than 24 breaths per minute, or oral temperature higher than 99.5 degrees Fahrenheit.

[66] Although some employees note that they feel cooler wearing icepack vests, there is some controversy regarding whether this type of equipment offers much real benefit.

that complies with the requirements outlined in OSHA's HAZWOPER standard 29 CFR 1910.120(f).

Hospital D has direct experience with employees who developed symptoms while treating a contaminated patient. The victim drank a quantity of organophosphate pesticide. During subsequent episodes of vomiting, the victim contaminated clothing, an ambulance, and the ED. As a result, six symptomatic staff members required hospitalization after exposure to the concentrated pesticide and vapor. The hospital followed its usual procedures for managing an employee with an occupational injury, including entering the illnesses in the OSHA Log of Work-Related Injuries and Illnesses (OSHA 300 Form, previously OSHA 200 Form) and ensuring workers' compensation medical leave for one affected individual.

Visual aids help communicate to hospital managers the advatages and possible location of proposed permanent decontamination systems.

Managing Employee Stress

Understandably, disasters can be a notable source of stress for anyone involved (Young et al., 2002; Hodgson et al., 2004). Hospital A points out that employee stress is a concern for decontamination teams and the hospital includes a mental health provider on each team. While assisting with decontamination activities, this employee also observes team members for symptoms of excessive stress. Additionally, Hospital A ensures decontamination team members have ready access to post-event counseling if they request such services.

RESPONSE
FACILITIES AND EQUIPMENT

Evaluating Existing Resources

Hospitals are challenged to identify spaces that will support decontamination activities (including equipment storage) and ensure operations can continue in the event one area of the hospital becomes contaminated. Hospitals planning additions or remodeling projects have a unique opportunity to design spaces appropriately. Other hospitals should use creative planning to identify existing architectural features that they can use to their advantage. Several examples follow:

- Hospital F has two existing physical characteristics that have proven advantageous: (1) in the event that one side of the ED became contaminated by an unannounced victim, doors between two sections of the ED can be closed and normal ED activities can continue on the uncontaminated side; and (2) a pair of unused, canopy-covered ramps leading to one entrance of the ER (left from a period of construction when the ER was used as the main entrance to the hospital) is being converted into a permanent decontamination shower for ambulatory patients. When considering use of divided spaces, hospitals should determine whether the ventilation systems are also separate and whether they recirculate air. If a space becomes contaminated, it might be necessary to shut down the area's ventilation system to prevent circulation of contaminated air to other spaces.

- While looking for an appropriate location for its large portable decontamination system, Hospital A (in a hot, humid climate) considered the advantages of a particularly large shade tree for preventing heat stress. The tree shades the entire shower system and all support features (extensive mechanical systems, triage and victim inspection stations, and victim waiting areas).

Isolation and Lockdown

The hospitals interviewed use a variety of methods to limit unauthorized access to the ED during emergencies until the victims have been decontaminated. The methods range from a guard with a key at the door to sophisticated keycard systems controlled at a central command center. The more complex systems tend to be associated with urban or recently modernized hospitals and are intended for use in any type of disturbance. Hospitals intend to use these methods if situations suggest that an unruly crowd will force its way into the hospital.

Decontamination

Equipment

Hospital A, which trains other hospitals to offer decontamination services, notes that it is critical to match the decontamination equipment purchased to the needs of the hospital and the community it serves. Hospital advisors recommend that any hospital with an emergency room should be prepared to decontaminate victims. However, facilities such as long-term care facilities and specialty clinics do not necessarily need decontamination capability. A hospital with a minimal risk of receiving multiple contaminated victims should consider acquiring a small system that can be handled by a few employees.[67] According to Hospital A, "every hospital should have a well-coordinated plan for arranging [timely] decontamination of any patients who may show up at the door, without putting staff at undue risk." The plan should include medical triage and treatment capability with proper precautions.

Although permanent decontamination systems have many advantages, portable facilities can be transported to other locations, if necessary.

Hospitals may select from an array of decontamination shower options. Portability is an advantage if the system might be required at different locations. A wide variety of portable, temporary decontamination systems are commercially available. Durable portable systems are designed to be cleaned and reused (if the type of contaminant is not highly toxic or persistent), while other systems are intended to be disposable and, thereby, simplify the post-incident recovery phase. The systems need to be stored in an easily

accessible location. There is considerable variety in the sizes of portable decontamination systems available and the number of people required to set up the system. All require some set-up time.

Permanent decontamination facilities are generally recommended over temporary equipment because these facilities can be activated quickly (some permanent models may be activated by simply unlocking the doors and turning on the water) and offer reliable long-term service. They also function well in harsh climates. Although permanent facilities require a dedicated space and more maintenance than disposable systems, Hospital A finds that permanent decontamination showers can generally be installed for the same (or lower) cost than a portable system with comparable features.

A blower can increase fresh air circulation through the decontamination system. In cold weather, the unit shown also heats air to a comfortable temperature.

Enclosed decontamination facilities should provide for fresh air circulation. When constructing a fully enclosed system, hospitals should consult a ventilation engineer or Certified Industrial Hygienist early in the system design phase.

Because of the time it takes first receivers to put on PPE and to set up decontamination facilities, hospitals may want to consider arranging for alternate rapid forms of decontamination until more sophisticated decontamination facilities are up and running. For example, some hospitals use high capacity, low-pressure hoses or showerheads, connected to high capacity, temperature-controlled water sources. These hoses and showers allow rapid preliminary drenching of multiple victims. Where multiple showerheads can be activated, ensure that the available water flow into,

---

[67] For example, a temporary shower facility with a wastewater collection device.

A roller system platform helps move non-ambulatory victims on backboards through the decontamination facility.

Hospitals can obtain military surplus equipment to supplement the decontamination facility supplies. (Shown here: a field stretcher for tranferring non-ambulatory victims from arriving vehicles to the decontamination facility.)

and through, the system is adequate to provide rapid decontamination at each showerhead.[68]

Hospitals A through G report that they considered the following factors when evaluating their decontamination system options:

- Previous experience with a particular system during drills or demonstration events. Characteristics that first receivers prefer include systems that are easily and rapidly set up by a minimal number of personnel and require little storage space.
- Compatibility with other equipment in the community (e.g., already owned by the fire department or other local organization). This feature allows systems to be joined to create a larger shower area. Additionally, more individuals in the community will be familiar with the system setup.
- Cost.
- Requirements prescribed by funding sources.
- Availability of space for a permanent shower.
- Community needs (anticipated frequency of use and required capacity).
- Need to operate the system in harsh weather.

Macintyre et al. (2000) suggest that the decontamination system should be operational within 2 to 3 minutes of notification of an incident. While this peri-

---

[68] To transfer water out of the shower area, hospitals use a portable electric pump (approximately 2.5 gallons per minute, or a rate similar to the standard combined water flow rate of the most consistently used showerheads; approved for submersion and on a ground-fault interrupt circuit). The pump sits in the shower base containment and pumps the accumulating wastewater into a portable rubber bladder or barrel. Wastewater storage barrels and bladders used by these hospitals range in size from 50 to 2,500 gallons capacity, and are selected based on the size of the decontamination system, anticipated average total water flow rate, and the number of victims the hospital is prepared to treat. While larger portable decontamination systems with multiple showerheads can generate wastewater more quickly than smaller systems, the large systems also tend to have larger floor-level water-containment enclosures.

od can be reasonable for some permanent decontamination facilities, realistically few temporary/portable systems can be activated that quickly. According to Hospital A, activation periods of 10 to 15 minutes are more typical for temporary decontamination facilities, even with highly trained and experienced staff. The hospitals interviewed for this site visit indicated that an inexperienced staff might require two to four times longer for set-up activities. Regular practice sessions and drills improve set-up teams' efficiency.

Regardless of the type of decontamination system selected, hospitals should avoid locating the decontamination facility *inside* the ED.

Additional information on evaluating and selecting decontamination equipment may be found at the Department of Veterans Affairs website http://www1.va.gov/vasafety/page.cfm?pg=291 and the National Institute of Justice website http://www.ojp.usdoj.gov/nij/pubs-sum/189724.htm.

Procedures

Decontamination procedures can have a large impact on first receiver exposure to hazardous substances. All the hospitals interviewed agree that the basic steps include:

1) Activate the EMP.
2) Learn as much as possible (as soon as possible) about the number of victims, the contaminant, and associated symptoms. Previous arrangements with first responder organizations can improve the timeliness and quantity of information received.
3) Activate the decontamination system and assemble the decontamination team and site security staff.
4) Perform any medical monitoring (e.g., vital signs), if specified by the EMP.
5) Put on PPE.
6) Triage victims to determine which individuals require decontamination and provide critical medical treatment to stabilize them before decontamination (e.g., atropine).
7) Assist victims (ambulatory and non-ambulatory) in removing contaminated clothing and securing personal property as soon as possible (within minutes of arrival).
8) Place clothing and other contaminated items in an approved hazardous waste container that is isolated outdoors so the items are not a continuing source of exposure.
9) Wash victims using soap, with good surfactant properties, and water (preferably tepid water to improve victim compliance). This step should include copious rinsing. [See discussion below.]
10) Inspect victims to evaluate the effectiveness of decontamination and guide decontaminated victims to the medical treatment area (Hospital Post-decontamination Zone). Return inadequately decontaminated victims to the shower area and repeat cleansing.
11) Decontaminate equipment and the decontamination system (if not disposable).
12) Staff remove PPE and decontaminate themselves.

See Appendix J for an additional example of victim decontamination procedures.

All of the steps above can influence the extent of healthcare workers' exposure to the contaminant. However, certain steps should be highlighted for their direct impact on the concentrations of contaminant first receivers will encounter. For example, disrobing might remove as much as 75 to 90 percent of the contaminant arriving on a victim (Macintyre et al., 2000; Vogt, 2002; USACHPPM, 2003a).[69] By isolating (in an approved hazardous waste container) the contaminated clothing, staff prevent these materials from off-gassing into the work area. To minimize first receiver exposure levels, these steps should be implemented immediately as victims arrive.

Non-ambulatory victims can require a substantial proportion of first receivers time and efforts. First receivers are likely to experience the greatest exposures while assisting these victims. Staff should take steps to identify possible sources of contamination and limit their exposure to those sources. For example, Hospital A uses specific procedures for removing victims clothing to minimize first receiver and victim exposures. Assistants use blunt-nose scissors to cut away clothing, rather than pulling it off. Tugging on clothing can produce a wringing action that might distribute contaminant on the victim, healthcare workers,

---

[69] The percentage of contaminant reduction depends on the type of clothing the victim was wearing when exposed. The estimates may be somewhat lower (down to 50 percent) for victims wearing short pants or skirts and higher (up to 94 percent) for victims exposed to biological warfare agents while wearing protective military uniforms (USACHPPM, 2003a).

and the surrounding area. Once removed, the clothing is immediately placed into a sealed container.

Unless a hospital uses detection equipment with demonstrated accuracy and reliability, victim washing procedures and visual inspection offer the only practical way healthcare workers can conclude that victims are definitively decontaminated. Staff in the ED might become exposed if contaminated victims are permitted to enter the Hospital Post-decontamination Zone. All the hospitals interviewed for this project indicated that they currently require victims to soap and shampoo completely and spend 5 to 6 minutes under a flow of running water. Some hospitals time the individual victims' total wash periods, while others observe the victims to ensure that they wash thoroughly. It may be advantageous to start the victim cleansing process with a full minute under a drenching shower to rinse away as much contaminant as possible, followed by subsequent soaping and rinsing steps, repeated as necessary (USACHPPM, 2003a). Hospital G has a progressive shower, in which each victim spends one minute at each of several wash stations.

Most of the hospitals interviewed also provide victims with written or pictorial instructions. In addition, tepid water, security of personal effects, single-gender facilities, shelter, and replacement clothing influence how quickly and completely victims comply with requirements to undress, shower appropriately, and wait for medical treatment until they are completely decontaminated. In cold climates, heated spaces and blankets might be necessary. Victim inspection provides a final check to ensure contaminant is not carried into the ED.

Victims from some incidents may arrive at the hospital after having been decontaminated at the incident site (Release Zone) or elsewhere. Before admitting a victim to the ED, first receivers should evaluate each individual to ensure the patient was adequately cleansed.

The methods staff use to decontaminate themselves and doff PPE also impact their own exposure. ATSDR, 2000 and Appendices K and L offer examples of procedures used by some hospitals. While there is little definitive published information available regarding optimal shower procedures (for victims or staff), the following sections summarize information provided by organizations with some expertise in this area. These procedures apply to a wide variety of contaminants and are appropriate for unknown contaminants that could arise from a release of toxic chemicals, bio-

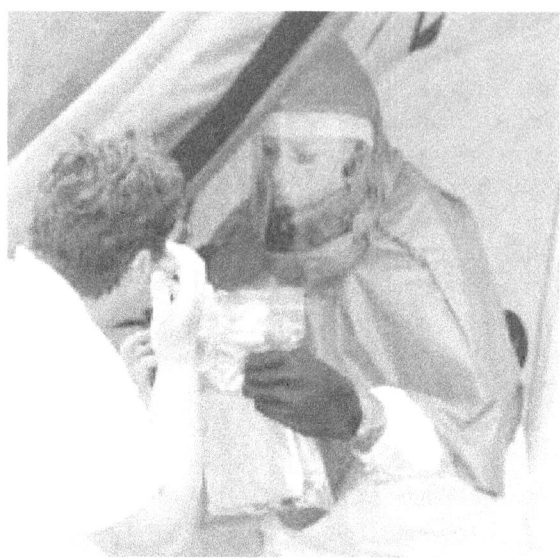

Put victim's personal items in a labeled plastic zip bag.

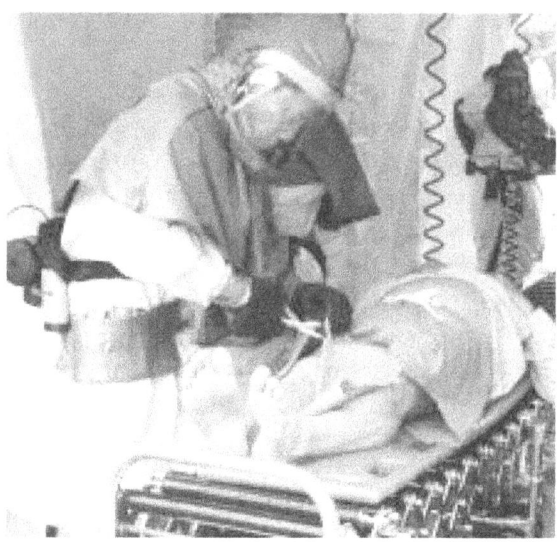

Use blunt scissors to cut away clothing. Avoid stretching or wringing cloth.

logical agents, or radiological particulates. Decontamination procedures, like PPE use, can be modified once the contaminant is identified; hospitals that are cleansing victims to remove known contaminants can tailor procedures as appropriate. For example, a longer rinse might be beneficial for corrosive substances or contamination in the eyes. Organizations such as the Center for Disease Control and Prevention (CDC) and the Department of Homeland Security offer specific recommendations for decontaminating victims exposed to individual hazards, such as ionizing radiation (CDC, 2003; Department of Homeland

Security, 2003).[70] After cleansing with soap and water, certain residual chemical warfare agents (sarin, mustard gas, and others) can be neutralized on the skin using a substance such as the reactive skin decontamination lotion (RSDL), used by the U.S. Army and other military organizations.[71]

Shower Flush Time and Practices

Numerous agencies and organizations recommend a shower time of approximately five minutes for contaminated victims brought to a hospital. Despite the fact that there is no empirical data, operational procedures deem this time as adequate.

- The U.S. Army Center for Health Promotion and Preventive Medicine (USACHPPM) recommends one-minute rinsing from head to toe with tepid water (slightly warm, not hot) after removal of contaminated clothing, followed by a more thorough decontamination of washing with a soap with good surfactant properties (e.g., hand dishwashing detergent), tepid water, and soft sponges. Avoid stiff brushes and vigorous scrubbing, which can damage the skin and increase the chance the contaminant would be absorbed by the victim. USACHPPM recommends these procedures for most classes of contaminants, except certain reactive metal dusts (USACHPPM, 2003a).

- The U.S. Army Soldier and Biological Chemical Command's (SBCCOM) Mass Casualty Decontamination Research Team (MCDRT) states that actual showering time will be an incident-specific decision but might be as long as 2 to 3 minutes per individual under ideal circumstances (SBCCOM, 2000b).

- The Agency for Toxic Substances and Disease Registry (ATSDR) recommends that patients contaminated with an unidentified chemical should flush exposed or irritated skin and hair with plain water for 3 to 5 minutes. For oily or otherwise adherent chemicals, mild soap on the skin and hair followed by a thorough rinse with water is also recommended (ATSDR, 2003).

- A technical expert for Hospital A's Emergency Mass-Casualty Decontamination Program stated that research regarding how long it takes to decontaminate an individual is scarce. This organization recommends a 5-minute shower time, based on operational experience. However, in some cases the total decontamination period could last longer than five minutes, depending on the agent, its viscosity, the quantity on the victim, and the amount of clothing removed.

Soap

Numerous agencies and programs recommend the use of water and a liquid soap with good surfactant properties (such as hand dishwashing detergent) to decontaminate victims during emergencies and mass casualties involving hazardous substances. Their recommendations are summarized here.

- SBCCOM's MCDRT recommends the rapid use of water, with or without soap, for decontamination. Using soap can marginally improve the results by ionic degradation of the chemical agent. Soap helps dissolve oily substances like mustard or blister agent. Liquid soaps are quicker to use than solids. However, the decontamination process should never be delayed to add soap (SBCCOM, 2000b).

- A multi-service effort of the U.S. Army, U.S. Marine Corps, U.S. Navy, and U.S. Air Force recommends that a contaminated individual use generous amounts of soap and water and scrub downward from head to toe. However, the decontamination process should not be delayed to due to a lack of soap (U.S. Army, 2001).

- A technical expert with Hospital A's Emergency Mass-Casualty Decontamination Program stated that this organization uses mild liquid (hand) dishwashing soap to avoid irritating the skin while still allowing, with enough water and friction, removal of the contaminant. He stated that the Department of Defense (DOD) has also suggested using mild soap for chemical warfare agents. USACHPPM suggests using mild (hand) dishwashing soap for removing a wide range of possible contaminants, including industrial chemicals, chemical warfare agents, biological agents, and radiological particles (USACHPPM, 2003a).

---

[70] The International Commission on Radiological Protection (ICRP) and the National Council on Radiation Protection and Measurement (NCRP) also offer guidance for radiological incidents.

[71] Neutralizing agents reduce toxic effects of agent already absorbed into the skin. RSDL won Food and Drug Administration (FDA) approval in 2003.

Security

Site security helps maintain order and control traffic around the decontamination facility and the hospital entrances. Security officers might need to control a contaminated individual to prevent other staff from becoming exposed and to protect equipment. Security officers also ensure contaminated victims do not bypass the decontamination hospital or enter the ED without passing inspection. In cases of civil disturbance, properly identified security officers protect the decontamination facility and staff so normal operations can continue.

Personal Protective Equipment

Hospitals should select PPE (e.g., respirators, suits, gloves, face and eye protection) based on a hazard assessment that identifies the hazards to which employees might be exposed. Under OSHA's Personal Protective Equipment standard (29 CFR 1910.132) or the parallel State Plan standards, all employers, including hospitals, must certify in writing that the hazard assessment has been performed. For first receiver PPE, hospitals may base the hazard assessment on the Personal Protective Equipment section of this best practices document, then use the PPE listed in Table 3. Hospitals likely to respond to incidents involving a specific hazard should adjust the PPE accordingly.

OSHA's Personal Protective Equipment standard also requires that employees be provided with equipment that fits appropriately. Some hospitals assign a set of protective equipment (except the PAPR respirator) to a specific individual. The equipment is stored in a container marked with the individual's name. Other hospitals maintain general supplies of PPE, storing sets of equipment by size (one set includes a large suit, large gloves, and large boots). In this case, the packages are clearly marked only with the size. Each first receiver tries on equipment to determine what size group fits best, then, during an emergency, the employee can quickly locate an appropriate PPE set. One hospital reported that boot size serves as the basis for its PPE sets. It is sometimes necessary to include two sizes of each type of glove in the set to ensure proper fit for everyone who wears the PPE set. Suits do not need to fit as closely and excess fabric can be taped or rolled to fit. To prevent protective suits from tearing at the crotch, hospitals should order over-sized suits (larger than the individuals normal size) (SBCCOM, 2003). Loose-fitting PAPR respirator

hoods offer a universal fit, thus are not included in individual or size-based PPE sets; however, tight fitting facepieces do require fit testing.

Hospitals must include first receivers' respirators in a respiratory protection program, as specified by OSHA's Respiratory Protection standard (29 CFR 1910.134), or the parallel State Plan standards. These respirators can be integrated into the hospitals existing respiratory protection program, which should include the following elements (listed in 1910.134(c)(1)):

- Procedures for selecting respirators for use in the workplace.
- Medical evaluations of employees required to use respirators.
- Fit testing procedures for tight-fitting respirators.
- Procedures for proper use of respirators in routine and reasonably foreseeable emergency situations.
- Procedures and schedules for cleaning, disinfecting, storing, inspecting, repairing, discarding, and otherwise maintaining respirators.
- Procedures to ensure adequate air quality, quantity, and flow of breathing air for atmosphere-supplying respirators.
- Training of employees in the respiratory hazards to which they are potentially exposed during routine and emergency situations.
- Training of employees in the proper use of respirators, including putting on and removing them, any limitations on their use, and their maintenance.
- Establishing and implementing respirator chemical cartridge change schedules.
- Procedures for regularly evaluating the effectiveness of the program.

Most of the hospitals interviewed for this project had previously developed respiratory protection programs covering the use of respirators by other employees. The hospitals were able to expand the program to include the use, cleaning, storage, and maintenance of the PAPRs worn by first receivers.

Certain materials absorb or are damaged by some chemical agents. As they become available, hospitals should select respirators that have been specifically tested for performance in the presence of chemical, biological, radiological, and nuclear hazards (CBRN). The National Institute for Occupational Safety and Health (NIOSH) is responsible for devel-

oping certification standards for approving various styles of CBRN respirators. When the HVA reveals a potential WMD threat and until NIOSH completes its CBRN certification process for PAPRs, use PAPRs that have been tested by the manufacturer for a CBRN environment.

NIOSH maintains a list of respirator makes and models certified for use against specific hazards or types of environments. Hospitals can search the list by contaminant type (e.g., organic vapors), facepiece style (e.g., hood) and other criteria. CBRN-approved respirators will appear on this list as they are certified. To access the list, see www.cdc.gov/niosh/nppt/topics/respirators/cel.

Protective equipment deteriorates with use and time. To minimize the amount of costly equipment expended during frequent drills, the interviewed hospitals typically maintain sets of PPE that are designated for drills. These "reusable" items are marked accordingly and repackaged after each training session. In differently marked containers, the hospitals store identical PPE (still in the original or comparable packaging) that would be used during a real incident.

Protective equipment storage can present challenges. The hospitals that were interviewed typically use one of two methods: cabinets or plastic storage boxes on shelves. Hospital A uses large stainless steel rolling cabinets that can be pushed to the ED entrance for easy equipment access when the decontamination facility is activated. Other hospitals use clear (easy to see contents) or colored (for coding) plastic storage containers to hold PPE sets and other supplies. To ensure that equipment is convenient during an emergency, the hospitals store equipment on shelves or cabinets near the ED door or in an adjacent room. One small hospital keeps equipment in locking cabinets along one wall of the small ED entry vestibule.

Long-term maintenance of battery-powered respirators, such as PAPRs, creates a special challenge. The batteries should be kept fully charged and should be maintained according to the manufacturer's directions. The respirator manufacturer's specific recommendations for charging, testing, and expected battery service life should be considered in any effort to maintain future readiness. Lithium-based batteries might offer more reliable long-term service. However, hospitals should discuss the relative merits and maintenance of the available batteries with the respirator manufacturer.

Staff can quickly move wheeled equipment carts from storage to the staging area.

A storage room near the ED door offers convenient access for first receivers' supplies.

Detection Equipment

Hospitals face a significant challenge in identifying contaminated individuals when they arrive unannounced as well as after decontamination procedures. All the hospitals interviewed depend on triage personnel or clerical staff to identify self-referred patients who have been in contact with hazardous substances. The first indication of the need to activate the hospital's EMP and decontamination team might come from staff who identify these individuals through an initial interview, by visual observation, by the presence of indicative odors, and through signs that a substance appears to be affecting health. After a victim has been through the decontamination system, hospitals rely on visual inspection and the extent to which the victim followed prescribed showering procedures. A few hospitals have access to commercially available detection equipment that can help with the identification. Although published selection criteria are available (see NIJ, 2000), the interviewed hospitals agree that the available practical detection equipment only evaluates specific hazards (e.g., ionizing radiation and traditional chemical weapon nerve and blister agents).[72]

Ionizing Radiation Meters

Experts suggest that alpha or beta emitting particles may be the more likely contaminants in mass casualty events involving the release of radiological particles (CDC, 2003). Relatively reliable and easy to use instruments are available for measuring ionizing radiation. Hospitals that offer patients nuclear medicine services generally have access to specific types of radiation meters used in that department. For example, the Radiation Safety Office for Hospital F indicated that such meters would be available for post-decontamination evaluation of victims, staff, and hospitals, as deemed appropriate. It is important that meters used by first receivers be selected based on the types of radiological particles with which victims could be contaminated.[73] To ensure more immediate access to appropriate equipment, Hospital B has obtained micro-roentgen per hour (μR/h) survey meters for the dedicated use of the decontamination team. In the event of a radiological emergency, the team will use the meters as they evaluate the effectiveness of victim decontamination.

To evaluate the effectiveness of decontamination procedures and also to help identify possible embedded fragments of radioactive materials, Hospital G obtained a pair of radiological monitoring devices (Ludlum Model 3 Survey Meters, with Model 44-7 End Window G-M Detectors and headphones). This choice was based on reports of good experiences with the instrument, price, and versatility (the equipment can be used for estimating exposure rate as well as detecting contamination). The hospital also acquired Radiagem-4 Personal Portable Radiometers, which are small hand-held gamma source meters that will potentially serve the dual purpose of screening victims for contamination and simultaneously recording

the accumulated exposure of the employee using the equipment. These user-friendly detectors integrate the reading and will alarm after reaching a preset threshold.[74]

Ionizing radiation detection equipment could also be useful for identifying contaminated individuals that might enter the ED unannounced. Hospital G is in the process of obtaining and testing radiation detection meters (Syrena Gamma Source Finder) that will be located at patient entrances to the hospital. These portable devices—about the size of an attaché case—will be tested at an entrance to determine whether they are useful for detecting radioactivity. The hospital hopes to use this type of equipment to avoid the spread of contamination by identifying contaminated individuals as they enter the hospital.[75] The hospital also plans to evaluate equipment that could be used to screen victims by moving them past an instrument (e.g., at the entrance and exit of a shower system) eliminating the need for an employee in this position.

Chemical and Biological Agent Detection Equipment

User-friendly equipment of adequate sensitivity is also becoming available for specific agents typically used as chemical weapons (Environmental Technologies, undated). For example, two of the interviewed hospitals (Hospitals B and C) obtained the same make and model ("APD 2000" from Environmental Technologies) of hand-held detection meters designed to detect parts per billion levels of specific chemical "nerve and blister agents" used as chemical weapons (e.g., organophosphates, and mustard agent).[76,77] However, a third hospital (Hospital A) felt that this type of equipment might be more useful for evaluating an incident site than for declaring victims to be thoroughly clean after decontamination efforts.

Equivalent equipment for detecting industrial chemicals and biological agents remains problematic. Although the interviewed hospitals indicated that they are interested in obtaining comparable detection

---

[72] Traditional chemical weapon nerve agents are commonly in the organophosphate chemical class.

[73] The U.S. Department of Homeland Security has adopted several standards for the design and performance criteria of radiation and nuclear detection equipment (see http://www.dhs.gov/dhspublic/display?content=3307).

[74] Hospital G also obtained a more costly portable spectrum analyzer that can also be used to measure ionizing radiation exposure rates. This instrument, which requires a skilled operator, might also be used to identify radioactive isotopes.

[75] In general, gamma source detectors are more useful for detecting a source of radiation, rather than for detecting contamination on an individual.

[76] The meter detects some agents at lower levels than others.

[77] The U.S. Armed Forces have also developed colorimetric contact paper to screen skin and equipment surfaces for these agents. However, the papers do not indicate potential for airborne exposures.

equipment that would identify and measure low levels of industrial chemicals or biological agents, none of the hospitals feel that the instruments *currently* available are practical for this purpose. Experts do agree, however, that some of the current broad-spectrum detection devices are capable of detecting classes of agents (although not the individual agent) with reasonable sensitivity and accuracy. Hospitals should determine the availability and utility of these instruments for the specific categories of substances identified in the hospital's HVA.

Hospital A indicated that optimal detection instruments would be (1) sensitive at low concentrations to a wide range of substances, (2) have a rapid response time (preferably a few seconds), (3) be easy to operate, (4) be rugged and portable enough to function outdoors under emergency conditions, (5) require only occasional routine maintenance, and (6) be reasonably priced. Macintyre et al., 2000, point out that the currently available detectors and monitors "would only complicate and lengthen the decontamination process," without providing substantial value.

TRIAGE CONSIDERATIONS

Hospital A notes that pre-decontamination triage serves three purposes:

- Distinguish contaminated individuals from other patients arriving at the hospital (e.g., by identifying symptoms and victim's proximity to a known chemical release).
- Identify victims who require immediate stabilization before they enter the decontamination system (e.g., shock and respiratory arrest).
- Identify injuries or critical pre-hospital treatment materials that will require special handling inside the decontamination system (e.g., a tourniquet that must be replaced with an uncontaminated compression device).

A plan for pre-decontamination triage should be included in the EMP.

Post-decontamination triage for medical treatment should occur in the Hospital Post-decontamination Zone, after victims are inspected and found to be free of contamination. Some hospitals combine decontamination and initial medical treatment (such as antidotes), which means either the healthcare worker attempts medical triage while wearing PPE (preferred) or the worker is at risk of exposure from victims that have not been adequately decontaminated.

EXTERNAL COMMUNICATION

Obtaining Timely Information

Experience has shown that hospitals cannot count on receiving immediate and complete information regarding an incident. However, hospitals can take steps to maximize their opportunities to receive useful and timely information. Hospitals D and F have found that the quality and timeliness of the received information improved as a result of strong working relationships with community organizations, coordinated EMPs, and drills conducted with other groups that respond to emergency situations.

Coordinating Activities

Coordinated response activities allow individual organizations to respond appropriately, when needed. Hospitals that work with the community to identify their roles can encourage coordinated responses. Hospital A (which maintains its own HAZMAT team in addition to a decontamination team) is located in a large urban area near other hospitals and fire departments, also with HAZMAT teams. As in many cities, the community's emergency management organization activates the appropriate HAZMAT team for each incident. This practice reduces the chance that response will be duplicated needlessly, thus protecting community resources that might otherwise be wasted. In the event that a large-scale emergency produced contaminated victims, Hospital A's two facilities (across a river from each other) would coordinate with the community to determine which one of its two decontamination locations to activate (based on number and location of victims)—or whether both systems would be required.

Hospitals should also activate two-way communication with the incident site. The more information a hospital can obtain regarding the hazard, the better first receivers will be able to protect themselves and treat the victims. Additionally, while treating victims, hospital staff might obtain valuable information regarding the nature of the contaminant, the route of entry, and symptoms of exposure. By passing these details back to the Release Zone, hospitals provide first responders at the site with information that could help those workers recognize possible signs of exposure, initiate life-stabilizing medical treatment, or adjust their PPE to provide better protection.

HOSPITAL DECONTAMINATION

Solid Waste Management

All hospitals consulted indicate that solid waste generated during victim decontamination activities will be treated as hazardous waste following the hospitals' existing hazardous waste management procedures. These hospitals plan to work with contract hazardous waste management companies to test and dispose of waste that is considered hazardous (except for any items required by law enforcement as evidence). Anticipating that the need might arise, several of the hospitals have made advance arrangements with private companies that specialize in hazardous waste removal.

For emergencies involving only a few contaminated victims, hospitals typically plan to use plastic bags to collect individual's contaminated clothing for disposal. The bags will be sealed and double-bagged or put in hazardous waste containers, then stored in existing secure hazardous waste storage areas until disposal. Hospitals that anticipate that they might receive a large number of contaminated victims maintain a supply of hazardous waste barrels (with airtight lids) into which decontamination team members will place contaminated materials. Hospital representatives stress that sealing the bags or closing the containers is important to eliminate contaminated materials as possible continuing sources of victim or health care worker exposure.

In response to some incidents, Federal authorities might request that certain types of waste be retained as evidence. In that case, the agency will provide instructions on handling the waste.

Wastewater Management

During an emergency, first receivers should take all necessary steps to save lives, protect the public, and protect themselves.[78] Once imminent threats to

human health and life are addressed, first receivers should make all reasonable efforts to contain contamination and avoid or mitigate environmental consequences (U.S. EPA, 2000).

Wastewater from decontamination showers can contain low-level concentrations of the substance(s) with which victims are contaminated. Given the opportunity to plan for decontamination activities (by designing and installing or purchasing decontamination facilities, developing procedures, and preparing staff), hospitals should consider the management of decontamination shower water as part of the plan. To determine appropriate wastewater management practices, hospitals should consult with LEPCs, whose members "can work together creatively using available resources to minimize the environmental impact of [hazardous materials] incidents" (U.S. EPA, 2000).

The hospitals interviewed follow several strategies for handling decontamination shower wastewater. Management methods range from complete water retention in a storage unit to uncontrolled release (e.g., into a parking lot or storm drain). The choice is usually based on the circumstances under which the individual decontamination system will be used. For example, these hospitals have generally arranged for some level of treatment or containment of wastewater generated by their primary decontamination systems (i.e., the systems that would be used most frequently). However, the same hospitals do not typically apply specific controls to wastewater from additional, open-air showerheads intended for use only as backup shower capacity (in the event that an unexpectedly large number of victims overwhelms the hospital's primary decontamination system).

Hospital B has a memorandum of understanding with the municipal wastewater treatment facility, which allows the hospital to drain water from its large, permanent, indoor decontamination system to the sanitary sewer. The agreement specifies that the hospital notify the treatment facility immediately when the shower is used to treat contaminated victims. Hospital B includes this notification in the EMP protocol for activating the shower.

Hospital A and Hospital C incorporate large (1,000 or more gallons) underground storage tanks into the design of their permanent, enclosed decontamination systems. When necessary, the water can be held until tested. After consultation with local environmental authorities, the hospital can either treat the wastewater, pump it out, or drain the water to the sanitary sewer or storm drain.

---

78   According to an EPA Alert (EPA, 2000), first responders' liability under the Comprehensive Environmental Response, Compensation, and Liability Act (CERCLA) for environmental damages occurring during hazardous materials incidents is limited (when public health or welfare are in danger) by the "Good Samaritan" provision contained in Section 107(d)(1) of CERCLA. This provision applies to emergencies involving hazardous materials release, including acts of terrorism. However, first responders also may be subject to liability based on applicable state statutes and regulations. Thus, first responders may consider consulting with local legal counsel to ascertain the scope of their potential liability. To access a copy of the EPA alert, see http://yosemite.epa.gov/oswer/Ceppoweb. nsf/vwResourcesByFilename/onepage.pdf/$File/onepage.pdf.

Among the hospitals interviewed, those that have obtained portable decontamination systems typically use a wastewater-containment device built into the base of the system enclosure. These containment devices usually include a low supportive wall (a few inches high) around the perimeter of the shower and a plastic lining to catch and hold wastewater. The hospitals often pump water from the shower base containment into a separate bladder to limit the volume in the shower base and to increase water storage capacity.[79] As with underground tanks, wastewater stored in bladders is held for subsequent testing and treatment or release, as deemed appropriate by authorities based on sample results.

An important consideration for positioning wastewater storage receptacles is the eventual need to drain or transport them (once filled, these containers are heavy and can only be shifted using special equipment). Hospital D noted that its hazardous waste management contractor provided useful advice about locating the wastewater receptacle where it could be easily accessed by the contractor's equipment, or could be drained with little assistance if water treatment was not required. This advice influenced the ultimate decontamination area design.

Decontaminating Surfaces and Equipment

The hospital EMP should include procedures for cleaning equipment and surfaces during and after an incident. Cleaning should be performed by properly protected and trained employees. Items that cannot be decontaminated safely should be processed for appropriate disposal. It is unlikely that portable gear could be adequately decontaminated after an incident involving a persistent or highly toxic agent.

The hospitals interviewed assign specifically trained individuals to be responsible for decontaminating and cleaning surfaces and equipment. These

individuals are usually members of the decontamination team, but at least one of the hospitals uses specially trained housekeeping or facilities management staff (hospital employees) to fill this role. It is important to note, however, that hospitals are increasingly concerned about delegating this role to housekeeping staff. According to the hospitals interviewed, the current industry trend is toward using contract services rather than hospital employees for general housekeeping activities. Hospital E acknowledged that for contracted employees, protection and liability issues can be complicated when contractual arrangements do not specifically address these matters. Additionally, rapid personnel turnover among contract housekeepers often hinders the hospital's ability to ensure workers receive specialized training.

Hospital D is considering a different contractual option. The hospital anticipates that large, time-consuming decontamination and associated recovery-phase cleaning tasks will be performed under contract by the hospital's hazardous waste service provider. This arrangement will include cleaning and/or disposal of the portable decontamination facility and equipment, and any areas of the ED that might become contaminated.

Employees of the *contract* hazardous waste service provider should be trained as required under 29 CFR 1910.120(b) through (o). If *hospital employees* perform the cleaning, appropriate training would either be that specified under 29 CFR 1910.120(q)(11), or 120 (b) through (o), depending on the situation *(this matter is currently under consideration by OSHA)*.

MAINTAINING FUTURE READINESS

To sustain a functional level of emergency preparedness, hospitals need to maintain equipment, supplies, and employee training. They should devote time and attention to evaluating and updating the HVA and EMP and coordinating these activities with the community. These efforts all require resources that will not be available without support at all levels of management. Hospitals D and F note that emergency planners can take active steps to help hospital management recognize the need for continuing effort. These steps might include providing management with after-action reports following drills and updated information regarding the community's expectations of the hospital.

Administrators need to be aware that all aspects of the EMP should be maintained equally. Continued

---

[79] To transfer water, hospitals use a portable electric pump (approximately 2.5 gallons per minute, or a rate similar to the standard combined water flow rate of the most consistently used showerheads; approved for submersion and on a ground-fault interrupt circuit). The pump sits in the shower base containment and pumps the accumulating wastewater into a portable rubber bladder or barrel. Wastewater storage barrels and bladders used by these hospitals range in size from 50 to 2,500 gallons capacity, and are selected based on the size of the decontamination system, anticipated average total water flow rate, and the number of victims the hospital is prepared to treat. While larger portable decontamination systems with multiple showerheads can generate wastewater more quickly than smaller systems, the large systems also tend to have larger floor-level water-containment enclosures.

employee training alone will not provide adequate protection if protective equipment (including respirator cartridges) is not replaced after use or when its shelf life expires. Some equipment, such as PAPR batteries, requires routine maintenance (e.g., charging and battery-life evaluation) for the life of the equipment. In addition, a well-maintained decontamination facility will not function well if employees do not have the experience of active, recent drills.

Hospitals in more mature stages of emergency management planning might require less concentrated efforts than during start-up, but continue to dedicate full- or part-time staff to ensure the hospital retains a full level of preparation. Emergency managers use creative methods to obtain additional help when needed. Hospital D uses an energetic emergency manager to direct the activities of employees from other departments who temporarily require light-duty work due to medical restrictions (after an illness or injury). These individuals provide some of the labor needed to update and improve the already-mature HVA and EMP.

Atmosphere supplying respirator (ASR):
A respirator that provides clean air from an uncontaminated source to the facepiece. Examples include supplied-air (airline) respirators, SCBA, and combination supplied-air/SCBA.

Assigned protection factor (APF):
A rating assigned to a respirator style by OSHA or NIOSH. This rating indicates the level of protection most workers can expect from the properly worn, maintained, and fitted respirator used under actual workplace conditions. An APF of 1,000 indicates that the concentration of contaminant inside the facepiece would be 1,000 times lower than the concentration in the surrounding air. A respirator with an APF of 1,000 will provide greater protection than a respirator with an APF of 100. (*Note: The APF should not be confused with a similar measure, the "fit factor," obtained during quantitative fit testing. Fit factors, which tend to be higher numbers, provide a relative indication of how well a respirator fits an individual, but do not represent the level of protection the respirator would provide in the workplace.*)

Awareness Level:
See First Responder Awareness Level.

CBRN:
Chemical, biological, radiological, or nuclear [agent or substance].

Clinicians:
Physicians, nurses, nurse practitioners, physicians' assistants, and others.

Doff:
To take off or remove (e.g., PPE).

Don:
To put on, in order to wear (e.g., PPE).

ED:
Emergency Department.

EMP:
Emergency Management Plan.

First Receiver:
Employees at a hospital engaged in decontamination and treatment of victims who have been contaminated by a hazardous substance(s) during an emergency incident. The incident occurs at a site other than the hospital. These employees are a subset of first responders .

First Responder:
Personnel who have responsibility to initially respond to emergencies. Some examples are firefighters, HAZ-MAT team members, law enforcement officers, lifeguards, forestry personnel, ambulance attendants, and other public service personnel. In the case of hazardous materials incidents, these personnel typically respond at the site where the incident occurred.

First Responder Awareness Level:
Individuals who might reasonably be anticipated to witness or discover a hazardous substance release and who have been trained to initiate an emergency response sequence by notifying the proper authorities of the release. They would take no further action beyond notifying the authorities. [OSHA HAZWOPER standard 29 CFR 1910.120(q)(6)(i)].

First Responder Operations Level:
Individuals who respond to releases or potential releases of hazardous substances as part of the initial response to the site for the purpose of protecting nearby persons, property, or the environment from the effects of the release. These individuals shall have received at least 8 hours of training or have sufficient experience to objectively demonstrate competency in specific critical areas. [OSHA HAZWOPER standard 29 CFR 1910.120(q)(6)(ii)].

HAZCOM:
OSHA's Hazard Communication standard [29 CFR 1910.1200].

HAZMAT:
Hazardous Material.

HAZWOPER:
OSHA's standard on Hazardous Waste Operations and Emergency Response, 29 CFR 1910.120. In particular, paragraph (q) of this standard covers employers whose employees are engaged in emergency response to hazardous substance releases.

Hazard Vulnerability Analysis (HVA):
The identification of potential emergencies and direct and indirect effects these emergencies may have on the healthcare organization's operations and the demand for its services.

Hazardous Substance:
Any substance to which exposure may result in adverse effects on the health or safety of employees. This includes substances defined under Section 101(14) of CERCLA (Superfund); biological or disease-causing agents that may reasonably be anticipated to cause death, disease, or other health problems; any substance listed by the U.S. Department of Transportation as hazardous material under 49 CFR 172.101 and appendices; and substances classified as *hazardous waste*.

Hospital Emergency Incident Command System (HEICS):
An example of an optional NIMS-based ICS tailored specifically for use by hospitals and designed to function in conjunction with other common ICSs used by emergency response organizations (e.g., Fire Service Incident Command System).

Hospital Decontamination Zone:
This zone includes any areas where the type and quantity of hazardous substance is unknown and where contaminated victims, contaminated equipment, or contaminated waste may be present. It is reasonably anticipated that employees in this zone might have exposure to contaminated victims, their belongings, equipment, or waste. This zone includes, but is not limited to, places where initial triage and/or medical stabilization of possibly contaminated victims occur, pre-decontamination waiting (staging) areas for victims, the actual decontamination area, and the post-decontamination victim inspection area. This area will typically end at the emergency department door. In other documents, this zone is sometimes called the "Warm Zone," "contamination reduction zone," "yellow zone," or "limited access zone."

Hospital Post-decontamination Zone:
The Hospital Post-decontamination Zone is an area considered uncontaminated. Equipment and personnel are not expected to become contaminated in this area. At a hospital receiving contaminated victims, the Hospital Post-decontamination Zone includes the emergency department (unless contaminated). This zone is sometimes called the "Cold Zone" or "Clean Area."

IDLH:
Or *Immediately dangerous to life or health,* means an atmospheric concentration of any toxic, corrosive or asphyxiant substance that poses an immediate threat to life or would interfere with an individual's ability to escape from a dangerous atmosphere.

Incident Command System (ICS):
A flexible organizational structure which provides a basic expandable system developed by Fire Services to mitigate an emergency situation of any size.

Incident Commander (IC):
The individual who holds overall responsibility for incident response and management.

JCAHO:
Joint Commission on Accreditation of Healthcare Organizations.

LEPC:
Local Emergency Planning Committee.

Mass Casualty:
"A combination of patient numbers and patient care requirements that challenge or exceed a community's ability to provide adequate patient care using day-to-day operations." (Barbera and MacIntyre, 2003).

NIMS:
The National Incident Management System, established by the U.S. Department of Homeland Security as a standardized management approach to incident response that all responders will use to coordinate and conduct response actions.

NFPA:
National Fire Protection Association.

Operations Level:
See First Responder Operations Level.

Personal Protective Equipment (PPE):
Examples include protective suits, gloves, foot covering, respiratory protection, hoods, safety glasses, goggles, and face shields.

Powered Air-Purifying Respirator (PAPR):
A respirator that uses a battery-powered blower to force air through a filter or purifying cartridge before blowing the cleaned air into the respirator facepiece.

Release Zone:
An area in and immediately surrounding a hazardous substance release. It is assumed to pose an immediate health risk to all persons, including first responders. For the purposes of this document, the Release Zone is always REMOTE from the hospital. This zone is also referred to as the "exclusion zone," the "red zone," and the "restricted zone" in other documents.

Self-contained Breathing Apparatus (SCBA):
A respirator that provides fresh air to the facepiece from a compressed air tank (usually worn on the worker's back).

Supplied-air Respirator (SAR):
A respirator that provides breathing air through an airline hose from an uncontaminated compressed air source to the facepiece. The facepiece can be a hood, helmet, or tight fitting facepiece.

Triage:
The process of screening and classifying sick, wounded, or injured persons to determine priority needs in order to ensure the efficient use of medical personnel, equipment, and hospitals.

WMD:
Weapon of Mass Destruction.

ACGIH. 2001. Heat Stress and Strain. Documentation of Threshold Limit Values and Biological Exposure Indices. American Conference of Governmental Industrial Hygienists (ACGIH), Cincinnati, OH.

ATSDR. 2000. Managing Hazardous Materials Incidents: Hospital Emergency Departments – A planning guide for the management of contaminated patients, Volume II (revised). Agency for Toxic Substances and Disease Registry, U.S. Department of Health and Human Services. Last accessed April 21, 2003: http://www.atsdr.cdc.gov/mhmi.html

ATSDR. 2003. Managing Hazardous Materials Incidents: Medical Management Guidelines (MMGs) for Unidentified Chemical, Volume III. Agency for Toxic Substances and Disease Registry, U.S. Department of Health and Human Services. Last accessed April 21, 2003: http://www.atsdr.cdc.gov/mmg.html

Auf der Heide, E. 2002. Principles of hospital disaster planning (Part II (8)). In Disaster Medicine. Hogan, D. and J.L. Burstein, editors. Lippincott Williams & Wilkins. Pp. 57-89.

Barbera, J.A., Anthony G. Macintyre. 2003. Mass Casualty Handbook: Hospital, Emergency Preparedness and Response, First ed. Jane's Information Group, Ltd.

Beatty, J. 2003. Decontamination procedures (personal e-mail correspondence). Central Arkansas Veterans Healthcare System, Little Rock, AR. October 23.

BNA. 2003. Hospitals low on protective suits in event of bioterrorist attack, report says. Daily Labor Report Banner, Bureau of National Affairs. August 13.

Burgess, J.L. 1999. Hospital Evacuations Due to Hazardous Materials Incidents. Am J Emerg Med 17:50-52. January.

CA EMSA. 2003a. Personal communication between Cheryl Starling of the California Emergency Medical Services Authority and Eastern Research Group, Inc. July 21.

CA EMSA. 2003b. Recommendations for Hospitals: Chemical Decontamination, Staff Protection, Chemical Decontamination Equipment and Medication List, Evidence Collection. Hospital and Healthcare System Disaster Interest Group (DIG). California Emergency Medical Services Authority. June.

CDC. 2003. Interim Guidelines for Hospital Response to Mass Casualties from a Radiological Incident. Centers for Disease Control and Prevention (CDC), U.S. Department of Health and Human Services. December.

Department of Homeland Security. 2003. Working document from Department of Homeland Security Working Group on Radiological Dispersal Devices (RDD) Preparedness Response Subgroup. Version: May 1.

DuPont. 2002. Technical Data Sheet. DuPont Tychem F: Helps protect against chemical warfare agents. E.I. DuPont de Nemours and Company.

DuPont. 2003. Permeation Guide for DuPont Tychem Protective Fabrics. E.I. du Pont de Nemours and Company.

ECRI. 2002. ECRI Advisor – Selecting personal protective equipment for chemical and bioterrorism preparedness: risks and costs. Center for Healthcare Environmental Management, Emergency Care Research Institute (ECRI), Plymouth Meeting, PA. March.

Environmental Technologies. (undated). Product literature for APD 2000. Environmental Technologies Group, Inc. Baltimore, MD.

Federal Register. 2003. Assigned Protection Factors; proposed rule. Occupational Safety and Health Administration (OSHA). 68 FR 34035. June 6.

Georgopoulos, P.G., P. Fedele, P. Shade, P.J. Lioy, M. Hodgson, A. Longmire, M. Sands, and M.A. Brown. 2004. Hospital response to chemical terrorism: personal protective equipment, training, and operations. American Journal of Industrial Medicine 46(5):432-445. November.

Goozner, B., L. Lutwick, E. Bourke. 2002. Chemical Terrorism: a Primer for 2002. Journal of the Association for Academic Minority Physicians. 13(1):14-18. January.

HCA. (undated). Disaster Readiness: Guidelines for Emergency Management Planners. Hospital Corporation of America (HCA). Nashville, TN.

HAZMAT for Healthcare. 2003. HazMat for Healthcare – An Operations Course. EnMagine, Diamond Springs, CA. Available at www.hazmatforhealthcare.org. Last accessed September 16.

Hendler et al. 2000. The Effect of Full Protective Gear on Intubation Performance by Hospital Medical Personnel. Military Medicine, Volume 149. [As cited in USACHPPM 2003a]

Hick, J. L., D. Hanfling, J.L. Burstein, J. Markham, A.G. Macintyre, J.A. Barbera. 2003a. Protective equipment for healthcare facility decontamination personnel: regulations, risks, and recommendations. Annals of Emergency Medicine 42(3):370-380. September.

Hick, J. L., P. Penn, D. Hanfling, M.A. Lapp, D. O'Laughlin, J.L. Burstein. 2003b. Establishing and training health care facility decontamination teams. Annals of Emergency Medicine 42(3):381-390. September.

Hodgson, M.J., A. Bierenbaum, S. Mather, M.A. Brown, J. Beatty, M. Scott, and P. Brewster. 2004. Emergency management program operational responses to weapons of mass destruction: Veterans Health Administration, 2001-2003. American Journal of Industrial Medicine 46(5):446-452. November.

Horton, D. K., Z. Berkowitz, W.E. Kaye. 2003. Secondary contamination of ED personnel from hazardous materials events, 1995-2001. Am J Emerg Med 21:199-204. May.

JCAHO. 2002. Guide to Emergency Management Planning in Health Care. Joint Commission Resources, Joint Commission on Accreditation of Healthcare Organizations, Oakbrook, IL.

JCAHO. 2004. Revised environment of care standards for the comprehensive accreditation manual for hospitals (CAMH). Joint Commission on Accreditation of Healthcare Organizations, Oakbrook, IL. Accessed April 21 at http://www.jcrinc.com/subscribers/perspectives.asp?durki=2515&site=10&return=1122

Koenig, K. 2003. Strip and shower: the duck and cover for the 21st Century. Annals of Emergency Medicine. 42(3): 391-394. September.

Lehmann, J. 2002. Considerations for selecting personal protective equipment for hazardous materials decontamination. Disaster Manag Response: 21-25. September.

Lundgren, R.E., A.H. McMakin. 1998. Risk Communications: A Handbook for Communicating Environmental, Safety, and Health Risks, Second ed. Columbus, OH: Battelle Press.

Macintyre, A.G., G.W. Christopher, E. Eitzen et al. 2000. Weapons of Mass Destruction Events with Contaminated Casualties: Effective Planning for Health Care Facilities. JAMA 283(2):242-249. January 12.

MMWR. 2001. Nosocomial poisoning associated with emergency department treatment of organophosphate toxicity – Georgia, 2000. Morbidity and Mortality Weekly, 49(51):1156-8. January 5.

NFPA. 2001. NFPA 1994 Standard on Protective Ensemble for Chemical/Biological Terrorism Incidents – 2001 Edition. National Fire Protection Association (NFPA), NY.

NFPA. 2002. NFPA 472 Standard for Professional Competence of Responders to Hazardous Materials Incidents. National Fire Protection Association (NFPA), NY.

NIJ. 2000. Guide for the Selection of Chemical Agent and Toxic Industrial Material Detection Equipment for Emergency First Responders – Volumes I & II (NIJ Guide 100-00). National Institute of Justice, U.S. Department of Justice. June. http://ncjrs.org/pdf-files1/nij/184449.pdf

NIOSH. 2003. NIOSH Pocket Guide to Chemical Hazards and Other Databases (online edition). National Institute for Occupational Safety and Health (NIOSH), Department of Health and Human Services (DHHS), Cincinnati, OH. Last accessed April 20, 2004 at: http://www.cdc.gov/niosh/npg/npg.html

Nozaki, H., S.O. Hori, Y. Shinozawa et al. 1995. Secondary exposure of medical staff to sarin vapor in the emergency room. Intensive Care Med 21:1032-1035. December.

Okumura, Takasu, Ishimatsu et al. 1996. Report on 640 victims of the Tokyo subway sarin attack. Annals of Emergency Medicine 28(2):129-135. August.

OSHA. 1991a. Letter of Interpretation Addressed to Mr. Edward McNamara, Executive Director, Central Massachusetts Emergency Medical Systems Corporation, Re: Training Requirements for emergency medical service personnel. June 14. Accessed April 6, 2004 at http://www.osha.gov/pls/oshaweb/owadisp.show_document?p_table=INTERPRETATIONS&p_id=20302

OSHA. 1991b. Letter of Interpretation Addressed to Mr. Eugene D. McCoy, Police Department, City of Ft. Lauderdale, FL. Re: Minimum number of hours required for awareness level for police officers. June 17. Accessed April 6, 2004 at http://www.osha.gov/pls/oshaweb/owadisp.show_document?p_table=INTERPRETATIONS&p_id=20307

OSHA. 1991c. Letter of Interpretation Addressed to Mr. William Borwegen, Service Employees International Union, AFL-CIO, Re: HAZWOPER EPA and OSHA jurisdictional issues. December 18. Accessed April 6, 2004 at http://www.osha.gov/pls/oshaweb/owadisp.show_document?p_table=INTERPRETATIONS&p_id=20500

OSHA. 1992a. Letter of Interpretation Addressed to Randy Ross, Re: Medical personnel exposed to patients contaminated with hazardous waste. March 31. Accessed April 6, 2004 at http://www.osha.gov/pls/oshaweb/owadisp.show_document?p_table=INTERPRETATIONS&p_id=20609

OSHA. 1992b. OSHA Letter of Interpretation from C.K. O'Toole to L. Bloomfield. Occupational Safety and Health Administration (OSHA), U.S. Department of Labor. Various questions on HAZWOPER. October 21. Accessed April 6, 2004 at http://www.osha.gov/pls/oshaweb/owadisp.show_document?p_table=INTERPRETATIONS&p_id=20890

OSHA. 1992c. Letter of Interpretation Addressed to Howard W. Levitin, Re: Training requirements for hospital personnel involved in an emergency response of a hazardous substance. October 27. Accessed April 6, 2004 at http://www.osha.gov/pls/oshaweb/owadisp.show_document?p_table=INTERPRETATIONS&p_id=20911

OSHA. 1993. Letter of Interpretation Addressed to Mr. Edward E. Hartin, Vice-President of Operations, HAZMAT Training Information Services, Inc., Re: Post-emergency response and medical surveillance requirements of HAZWOPER. August 5. Accessed April 6, 2004 at http://www.osha.gov/pls/oshaweb/owadisp.show_document?p_table=INTERPRETATIONS&p_id=21222

OSHA. 1997. Letter of Interpretation Addressed to Mr. Thomas Whittaker, New England Hospital Engineer's Society, Re: Emergency response training requirements for hospital staff. April 25. Accessed April 6, 2004 at http://www.osha.gov/pls/oshaweb/owadisp.show_document?p_table=INTERPRETATIONS&p_id=22393

OSHA. 1999. Letter of Interpretation Addressed to Daniel Burke, Safety Coordinator, St. John's Medical Center, Re: Emergency response training necessary for hospital physicians/nurses that may treat contaminated patients. March 10. Accessed April 6, 2004 at http://www.osha.gov/pls/oshaweb/owadisp.show_document?p_table=INTERPRETATIONS&p_id=22710

OSHA. 2002a. Letter of Interpretation Addressed to Mr. Francis J. Roth, Supervisor, Loss Protection, Princeton Insurance, Re: Level of respiratory protection required for hospital staff members. September 5. Accessed April 6, 2004 at http://www.osha.gov/pls/oshaweb/owadisp.show_document?p_table=INTERPRETATIONS&p_id=24516

OSHA. 2002b. Letter of Interpretation Addressed to Captain Kevin J. Hayden, Acting Commanding Officer, State of New Jersey Emergency Management Section, Re: Personal protective requirements for hospital employees. December 2. Accessed April 6, 2004 at http://www.osha.gov/pls/oshaweb/owadisp.show_document?p_table=INTERPRETATIONS&p_id=24523

OSHA. 2002c. Memorandum for Regional Administrators (RAs) regarding enforcement policy change for respiratory protection for select respirators for use in the pharmaceutical industry. May 30. Accessed April 6, 2004 at http://www.osha.gov/pls/oshaweb/owadisp.show_document?p_table=INTERPRETATIONS&p_id=24248

OSHA. 2003. Letter of Interpretation Addressed to Mike Bolt, Re: HAZWOPER training requirements for hospital staff who decontaminate chemically contaminated patients. April 22. Accessed April 6, 2004 at http://www.osha.gov/pls/oshaweb/owadisp.show_document?p_table=INTERPRETATIONS&p_id=24605

Penn P. 2002. Hospital Hazardous Material Emergency Response: The Devil is in the Details. National Disaster Medical Systems Conference. Atlanta, GA. April 14.

San Mateo County HAS. 1998. HEICS – The hospital emergency incident command system (Volumes I and II). San Mateo County Health Services Agency. June. Accessed August, 2003 at www.emsa.cahwnet.gov.

Saruwatari. 2003. Personal communication between M. Saruwatari of Kaiser Permanente, and Eastern Research Group, Inc. August 18.

SBCCOM. 2000a. Guidelines for Responding to a Chemical Weapons Incident. Domestic Preparedness Chemical Team, U.S. Army Soldier and Biological Chemical Command. http://transit-safety.volpe.dot.gov/training/Archived/EPSSeminarReg/CD/documents/Weapons/cwirp_guidelines.pdf

SBCCOM. 2000b. Guidelines for Mass Casualty Decontamination During a Terrorist Chemical Agent Incident. U.S. Army Soldier and Biological Chemical Command. January. http://transit-safety.volpe.dot.gov/security/SecurityInitiatives/Top20/1 -- Management and Accountability/3A -- Integrated System/Additional/SBCCOM_Guidelines_for_Mass_Casualty_Decon.pdf

SBCCOM. 2001a. Swatch Test Results of Commercial Chemical Protective Gloves to Challenge by Chemical Warfare Agents: Executive Summary. Domestic Preparedness Chemical Team, U.S. Army Soldier and Biological Chemical Command. February. http://www.edgewood.army.mil/downloads/reports/protective_gloves_summary_report.pdf

SBCCOM. 2001b. Swatch Test Results of Phase 2 Commercial Chemical Protective Gloves to Challenge by Chemical Warfare Agents: Executive Summary. Domestic Preparedness Chemical Team, U.S. Army Soldier and Biological Chemical Command. June. http://www.edgewood.army.mil/downloads/reports/protective_gloves_phase2_ca.pdf

SBCCOM. 2003. Guidelines for Use of Personal Protective Equipment by Law Enforcement Personnel During a Terrorist Chemical Agent Incident. U.S. Army Soldier and Biological Chemical Command. Original June 2001. Revised July 2003. http://www.edgewood.army.mil/downloads/cwirp/ppe_law_enforcement_ca_incident.pdf

Schultz, M., J. Cisek, and R. Wabeke. 1995. Simulated exposure of hospital emergency personnel to solvent vapors and respirable dust during decontamination of chemically exposed patients. Annals of Emergency Medicine. 26(3):324-329. September.

Sutter Health. 2002. Training materials: First Responder Operations. Sutter Health, Sacramento, CA. October 1.

Thorne, C. D., Curbow B., Oliver M. et al. 2003. Terrorism preparedness training for nonclinical hospital workers: empowering them to take action. J Occup Environ Med 45:333-337. March.

U.S. EPA. 2000. First responders' environmental liability due to mass decontamination runoff (EPA 550-F-00.009). U.S. Environmental Protection Agency, Office of Solid Waste and Emergency Response. July. http://yosemite.epa.gov/oswer/Ceppoweb.nsf/vwResourcesByFilename/onepage.pdf/$File/onepage.pdf

USACHPPM. 2003a. Personal Protective Equipment Guide for Military Medical Treatment Facility Personnel Handling Casualties from Weapons of Mass Destruction and Terrorism Events (Technical Guide 275). U.S. Army Center for Health Promotion and Preventive Medicine. August. http://chppm-www.apgea.army.mil/documents/TG/TECHGUID/TG275new.pdf

USACHPPM. 2003b. Chemical Risk Assessment and Exposure Guidelines (and how AEGLs fit in). U.S. Army Center for Health Promotion and Preventive Medicine, Directorate of Health Risk Management. March. http://www.osha.gov/SLTC/emergencypreparedness/chemical/ppt/csepp-aegl_march_2003.ppt.

U.S. Army, U.S. Marine Corps, U.S. Navy, and U.S. Air Force. 2001. Multiservice Tactics, Techniques, and Procedures for Nuclear, Biological, and Chemical Aspects of Consequence Management. AFTTP (I) 3-2.37. December.

VA. 2003. VHA Decontamination Training Program – Train the Trainer Participant Manual. Little Rock Employee Education Resource Center, Employee Education System, Department of Veterans Affairs (VA), Little Rock, AR. April.

Vogt, B.M. and J.H. Sorrensen. 2002. How clean is safe? Improving the effectiveness of decontamination of structures and people following chemical and biological incidents – Final Report (ORNL/TM-2002/178). Prepared by Oakridge National Laboratory for the U.S. Department of Energy. October. Accessed September 2004 at http://emc.ornl.gov/EMCWeb/EMC/PDF/How_Clean_is_Safe.pdf

Walter, F. G., Bates, G., Criss, E. A. et al. 2003. Hazardous materials responses in a mid-sized metropolitan area. Prehosp Emerg Care 7:214-218. Apr-Jun.

Young, Bruce H., Ford, Julian D., Rusek, Josef I. et al. Disaster Mental Health Services: A Guidebook for Clinicians and Administrators. National Center for PTSD. Last Accessed: 2002. Available from: http://www.ncptsd.org/treatment/disaster/index.html.

Agency for Toxic Substances and Disease Registry
www.atsdr.cdc.gov

Agency for Toxic Substances and Disease Registry, Division of Regional Operations
http://www.atsdr.cdc.gov/DRO

California Emergency Medical Services Authority
www.emsa.ca.gov

Centers for Disease Control and Prevention (CDC)
http://www.cdc.gov/

Department of Veterans Affairs
http://www1.va.gov/vasafety/page.cfm?pg=528

Healthcare Association of Hawaii
www.hah-emergency.net

Homeland Security
http://www.whitehouse.gov/homeland/

The InterAgency Board
http://www.iab.gov/

Joint Commission on Accreditation of Healthcare Organizations
www.jcaho.org

Local Emergency Planning Committee (LEPC) Locations
www.epa.gov/swercepp/lepclist.htm

DisasterHelp (U.S. Office of Management and Budget – Disaster Management Initiative)
https://disasterhelp.gov/portal/jhtml/index.jhtml

National Institute of Justice
www.ojp.usdoj.gov/nij

National Institute for Occupational Safety and Health (NIOSH)
http://www.cdc.gov/niosh/homepage.html

Occupational Safety and Health Administration (OSHA) [includes contact information for OSHA-approved State Plans]
www.osha.gov

Office for Domestic Preparedness
http://www.ojp.usdoj.gov/odp/welcome.html

U.S. Army Center for Health Promotion and Preventive Medicine (USACHPPM)
http://chppm-www.apgea.army.mil/

U.S. Army Medical Institute for Chemical Defense, Chemical Casualty Care Division
https://ccc.apgea.army.mil/

U.S. Army Soldier and Biological Chemical Command
(Effective 9 October 2003, SBCCOM has been re-designated). See sites below:

Research, Development and Engineering Command (RDECOM)
http://www.rdecom.army.mil/

Chemical Materials Agency (CMA)
http://www.cma.army.mil/

PM Nuclear, Biological and Chemical Defense (PM NBC)
http://www.pmnbc.army.mil/

Soldiers System Center (SSC)
http://www.natick.army.mil/

FACEPIECE STYLE	ADVANTAGES	DISADVANTAGES
Half facepiece	• Employee may wear any appropriate eyewear that does not interfere with the respirator seal.	• If there is a break in the seal between the mask and the face, contaminated air can enter. Fit testing must be performed prior to use and user seal checks must be done by the user every time the respirator is used. • Does not provide eye protection.
Full facepiece	• When used with a powered air-purifying respirator (PAPR), a tight fitting facepiece might allow a worker to pull filtered air into the facepiece if the battery fails. • Provides eye protection.	• If there is a break in the seal between the mask and the face, contaminated air can enter. Fit testing must be performed prior to use and user seal checks must be done by the user every time the respirator is used. • Workers who wear glasses may require spectacle kits to be used inside the facepiece.
Loose fitting helmet/hood	• Provides eye protection. • Provides skin protection for the head and (certain models) neck. • Fit testing is not required. • Some workers find loose fitting respirators more comfortable than tight fitting models. • Can be worn by employees with facial hair and facial scars/deformities. • Employees may wear their own glasses under the helmet/hood.	• When used with a PAPR, the hood will provide little or no protection if the battery fails.

Adapted from *Personal Protective Equipment Guide for Military Medical Treatment Facility Personnel Handling Casualties from Weapons of Mass Destruction and Terrorism Events* (Technical Guide 275). U.S. Army Center for Health Promotion and Preventive Medicine (USACHPPM), August 2003.

Note: This appendix provides a brief look at the general format two healthcare organizations use as the basis for their HVAs. Contact the Joint Commission on Accreditation of Healthcare Organizations (JCAHO) for more information, including additional format examples, instructions for completing HVAs, and lists of the types of events that might be included in an HVA.

Example 1.
Kaiser Permanente Hazard Vulnerability Analysis

This document is a sample Hazard Vulnerability Analysis tool. It is not a substitute for a comprehensive emergency preparedness program. Individuals or organizations using this tool are solely responsible for any hazard assessment and compliance with applicable laws and regulations.

Instructions

Evaluate potential for event and response among the following categories using the hazard specific scale. Assume each event/incident occurs at the worst possible time (e.g., during peak patient loads). Please note specific score criteria on each worksheet to ensure accurate recording.

Issues to consider for **probability** include, but are not limited to:
1. Known risk
2. Historical data
3. Manufacturer/vendor statistics

Issues to consider for **response** include, but are not limited to:
1. Time to marshal an on-scene response
2. Scope of response capability
3. Historical evaluation of response success

Issues to consider for **human impact** include, but are not limited to:
1. Potential for staff death or injury
2. Potential for patient death or injury

Issues to consider for **property impact** include, but are not limited to:
1. Cost to replace
2. Cost to set up temporary replacement
3. Cost to repair
4. Time to recover

Issues to consider for **business impact** include, but are not limited to:
1. Business interruption
2. Employees unable to report to work

3. Customers unable to reach facility
4. Company in violation of contractual agreements
5. Imposition of fines and penalties or legal costs
6. Interruption of critical supplies
7. Interruption of product distribution
8. Reputation and public image
9. Financial impact/burden

Issues to consider for **preparedness** include, but are not limited to:
1. Status of current plans
2. Frequency of drills
3. Training status
4. Insurance
5. Availability of alternate sources for critical supplies/services

Issues to consider for **internal resources** include, but are not limited to:
1. Types of supplies on hand/will they meet need?
2. Volume of supplies on hand/will they meet need?
3. Staff availability
4. Coordination with any medical office buildings (e.g., doctors' offices and clinics) included in the EMP
5. Availability of back-up systems
6. Internal resources ability to withstand disasters/survivability

Issues to consider for **external resources** include, but are not limited to:
1. Types of agreements with community agencies/drills
2. Coordination with local and state agencies
3. Coordination with proximal (close by) healthcare facilities
4. Coordination with treatment-specific facilities
5. Community resources

Complete all worksheets including Natural, Technological, Human and Hazmat. The summary section will automatically provide your specific and overall relative threat.

Sources:
Kaiser Permanente.
American Society for Healthcare Engineering (ASHE, 2000).

EXAMPLE 1. KAISER PERMANENTE HAZARD VUNUERABILITY ANALYSIS
HAZARD AND VULNERABILITY ASSESSMENT TOOL
(example of format used with a complete threat list)

TECHNOLOGIC EVENTS   **RISK = PROBABILITY * SEVERITY**

SEVERITY = (MAGNITUDE - MITIGATION)

EVENT	PROBABILITY	HUMAN IMPACT	PROPERTY IMPACT	BUSINESS IMPACT	PREPARED-NESS	INTERNAL RESPONSE	EXTERNAL RESPONSE	RISK
	Likelihood this will occur	*Possibility of death or injury*	*Physical losses and damages*	*Interruption of services*	*Preplanning*	*Time, effectivness, resources*	*Community/ mutual aid staff and supplies*	*Relative threat*[§]
SCORE	*0 = N/A* *1 = Low* *2 = Moderate* *3 = High*	*0 = N/A* *1 = Low* *2 = Moderate* *3 = High*	*0 = N/A* *1 = Low* *2 = Moderate* *3 = High*	*0 = N/A* *1 = Low* *2 = Moderate* *3 = High*	*0 = N/A* *1 = High* *2 = Moderate* *3 = Low-none*	*0 = N/A* *1 = High* *2 = Moderate* *3 = Low-none*	***0 = N/A*** ***1 = High*** ***2 = Moderate*** ***3 = Low-none***	*0 - 100%*
Mass Casualty Incident (trauma)								
Terrorism, Biological								
Mass Casualty Incident (medical/infectious)								
Fuel Shortage								
Natural Gas Failure								
Water Failure								
Sewer Failure								
Steam Failure								
Fire Alarm Failure								
Communications Failure								
Medical Vacuum Failure								
HVAC Failure								
Information Systems Failure								
Fire, Internal								
Hazmat Exposure, Internal								
AVERAGE SCORE								

[§]*Threat increases with percentage.*

EXAMPLE 2. NEW YORK UNIVERSITY MEDICAL CENTER
HAZARD VUNERABILITY ANALYSIS
Version date: August 2003

Instructions
Evaluate each potential event with respect to the probability, risk, and the perceived level of preparedness. Add additional events as needed.

Issues to consider for **probability** include, but are not limited to:
1. Known Risk
2. Historical Data
3. Manufacturer/Vendor Statistics
4. Intelligence Information from Law Enforcement

Issues to consider for **risk** include, but are not limited to:
1. Immediate Danger (Threat) to Life or Health (IDLH)
2. Disruption of Services
3. Damage/Failure Potential
4. Loss of Community Trust
5. Financial Impact
6. Legal Issues

Issues to consider for **preparedness** include, but are not limited to:
1. Status of Current Plans
2. Training Status
3. Insurance
4. Availability of Back-up Systems
5. Community Resources

Computation
The event score is arrived at by multiplying each of the ratings (Probability * Risk * Preparedness). The total values in descending order represent the event in need of organization focus and resources for emergency planning. The organization needs to determine a value below which no action is required.

(Example of format used with a threat list)
(Version date: August 2003)

EVENT	PROBABILITY				RISK					PREPAREDNESS			TOTAL
	HIGH	MED	LOW	NONE	Life Threat	Health/ Safety	High Disruption	Moderate Disruption	Low Disruption	POOR	FAIR	GOOD	
Score	3	2	1	0	5	4	3	2	1	3	2	1	
Mass Casualty Incident (MCI) (Trauma)													
MCI (Medical)													
MCI (HazMat)													
Small Scale HazMat													
Terrorism Chemical													
Terrorism Biological													
Terrorism Nuclear													

ABOUT THE HEICS III PROJECT

In 1992, a generic disaster response plan was released to hospitals based upon the Incident Command System. *The Hospital Emergency Incident Command System*, modeled after the FIRESCOPE management system, was first tested by six hospitals in Orange County, California. A second edition was developed by a state-wide task force and tested again by Orange and Los Angeles County hospitals. In May 1992, the Second Edition of the Hospital Emergency Incident Command System (HEICS) was made available with copies having been sent throughout the United States, Canada, and across the globe.

HEICS features a flexible management which allows for a customized hospital response to the crisis at hand. There is an organizational chart with forty-nine positions grouped into one of four sections. This all results in an organized division of tasks and a realistic span of control for each manager. This organizational structure provides a platform for common terminology to enhance communication and improve documentation.

Following the 1993 Northridge Earthquake, HEICS was used successfully by some hospitals damaged in the quake. The plan has also been used in single hospital emergencies and in many disaster exercises. From these repeated uses of the HEICS program, much insight has been gained. It is the goal of San Mateo

County Emergency Medical Services that the Hospital Emergency Incident Command System Update Project recreate a HEICS plan which is more useful and relevant to the medical community. And, a plan which is more accessible, as is found in this website (www.emsa.ca. gov). You are invited to access and download the Second Edition of the HEICS plan. You are encouraged to take a critical look at this document and return your comments to the San Mateo County Emergency Medical Services team who are working on this exciting update.

For More Information...

about the Hospital Emergency Incident Command System, contact the California Emergency Medical Services Authority at (916) 322-4336; or visit the website at www.emsa.ca.gov. Electronic copies of the materials contained in this appendix are available from the EMSA website.

Source:
California Emergency Medical Services Authority, Sacramento.

HOSPITAL EMERGENCY INCIDENT COMMAND SYSTEM

Third Edition

EXECUTIVE SUMMARY

January 1998

Confusion and chaos are commonly experienced by the hospital at the onset of a medical disaster. However, these negative effects can be minimized if management responds quickly with structure and a focused direction of activities. **The Hospital Emergency Incident Command System (HEICS)** is an emergency management system which employs a logical management structure, defined responsibilities, clear reporting channels, and a common nomenclature to help unify hospitals with other emergency responders. There are clear advantages to all hospitals using this particular emergency management system.

Based upon public safety's Incident Command System, HEICS has already proved valuable in helping hospitals serve the community during a crisis and resume normal operations as soon as possible. A survey of California hospitals in the Spring of 1997, revealed that a significant number of hospitals have, or will be incorporating HEICS within their emergency plans. HEICS is fast becoming the standard for health care disaster response and offers the following features:

- **predictable** chain of management
- **flexible organizational chart** allows **flexible response** to specific emergencies
- **prioritized response checklists**
- **accountability** of position function
- **improved documentation** for improved accountability and cost recovery
- **common language** to promote communication and facilitate outside assistance
- **cost-effective emergency planning** within health care organizations

The 1996 Edition of the National Fire Protection Association, *Health Care Facilities Handbook* states in chapter 11-4.3, "The disaster planning committee shall model the disaster plan on the incident command system (ICS)." The American Society for Healthcare Engineering of the American Hospital Association in an August 1997 *Healthcare Facilities Management Series* states "One of the best examples of emergency pre-paredness through checklists can be found in The Hospital Emergency Incident Command System..." **In California, public hospitals seeking financial recovery following a declared disaster are required to implement the 1993 mandates of the Standardized Emergency Management System.** The utilization of the HEICS plan is recognized as partial compliance with this state law.

HEICS and all of its support material is offered without charge. Implementation templates and instructional materials are free and make the cost of converting to the HEICS system minimal. HEICS is financially prudent as it assists the medical facility in staying open following a disaster and promotes the restoration of day-to-day hospital functions. It is an efficient method for managing emergencies of disastrous proportions, as well as those of a lesser degree.

ORGANIZATIONAL CHART

- **Positions may or may not be activated.**

  Each emergency must be evaluated as to the specific positions which will need activation in order to address challenges of the emergency. The disaster's nature, proximity, and other factors may mandate all or very few of the positions to be staffed.

- **Positions may be filled immediately or later based upon needs and staffing.**

  A particular disaster may require that a certain number of positions need to be filled. However, if there are only a few managers available for the next 12 hours, then each manager must take more than one position. If this is not acceptable, then the top priority positions must be identified and carried out in the best manner possible.

- **More than one position may be assigned to an individual.**

  Many managers are capable of carrying out more than one function at a time. Situations of a critical nature may require an individual to perform multiple tasks until additional support can be obtained. The use of checklists should facilitate the task of multiple position assignment.

Note: HEICS does not formally incorporate a decontamination team; however, "decontamination team leader" might be included under "treatment area supervisor" or other operational subgroup. If the hospital actually has a HAZ-MAT release response team, this may be a separate operational subunit.

Hospital Emergency Incident Command System Organization Chart

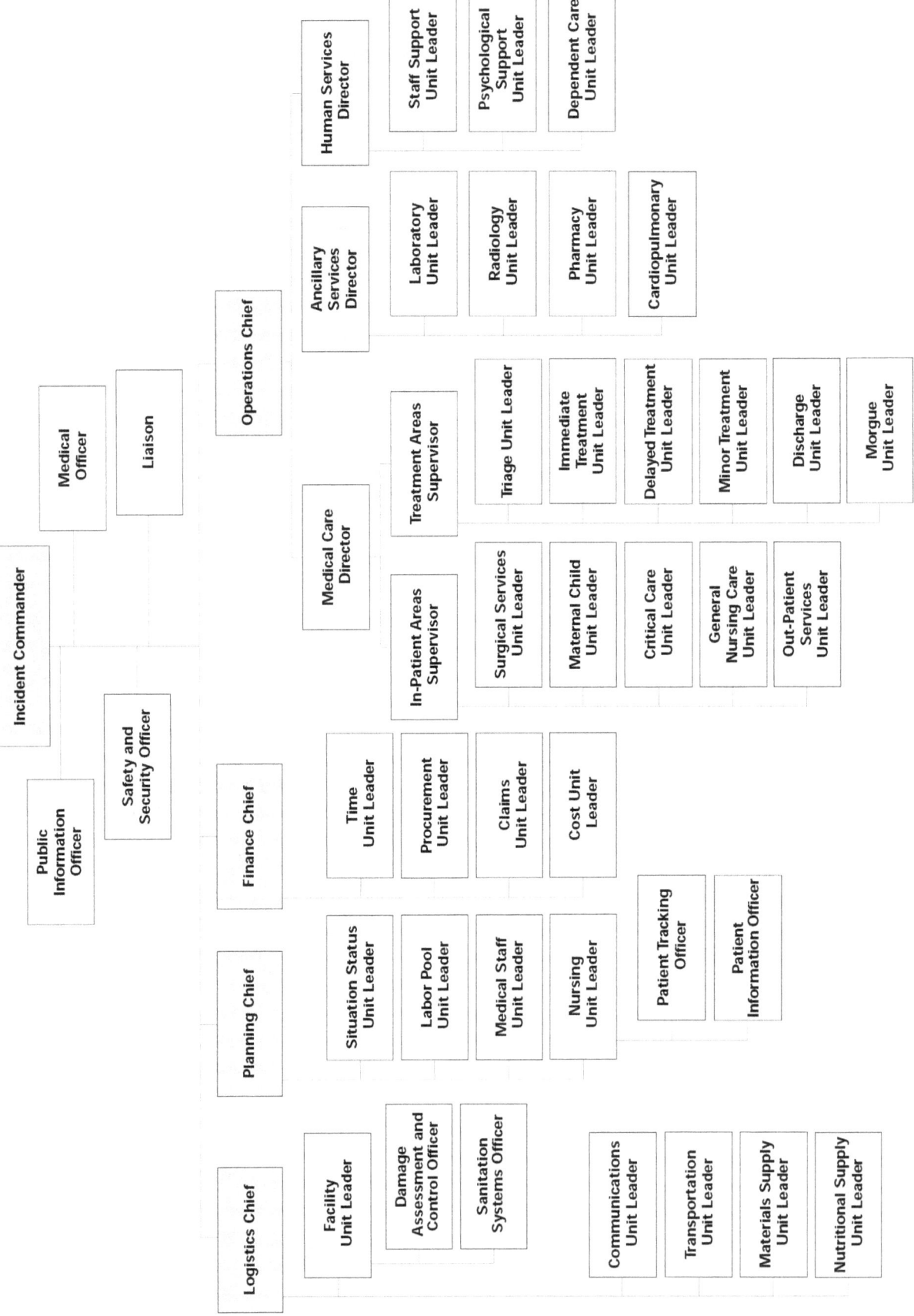

Example 1. NVERC Medical Monitoring of Response Staff

Northern Virginia Emergency Response Coalition

It is important to determine that personnel who are being asked to wear personal protective equipment (PPE) during a hazmat/weapon of mass destruction (WMD) incident have no preexisting medical conditions that might put them at increased risk for illness or injury. The following medical monitoring procedure is to be used from the outset of an incident to accomplish this objective.

At the Outset of the Incident

- The medical monitoring equipment (blood pressure [BP] cuffs, stethoscopes, scales, thermometers, medical monitoring sheets) should be brought from the PPE storage area and placed in the PPE dress out area.
- 1–2 staff persons should be assigned responsibility to perform medical monitoring of all response personnel.
- Time permitting (ex. advance incident information and arrival notice has been given by emergency medical services [EMS]), each person intending to dress in PPE is to have the following pre-entry medical monitoring assessment completed and recorded on their Medical Monitoring Incident Response Record:
  - BP
  - Pulse
  - Respirations
  - Weight
  - Temperature
  - Listing of current medications
  - Confirmation of no current, upper respiratory tract infection, chronic obstructive pulmonary disease, sinusitis, or gastrointestinal illness.
- If there is inadequate time to perform pre-entry medical monitoring it will be important that each staff member exercises good judgment and dress out only if they know there is no preexisting condition that should preclude their use of PPE.

Sources:

Northern Virginia Emergency Response Coalition. Available at: http://www.hazmatforhealthcare.org/download/doc/misc Patient_Decontamination_Procedure-complete.doc (Accessed September 2, 2003).
NIOSH Publication No. 86-112 "Working in Hot Environments."

- The clinical data obtained from medical monitoring done on each person must fall within the participation criteria listed. Persons whose vital signs exceed the requirements should either be sent to rest for 15–30 minutes and then re-examined or given a responsibility not requiring the use of PPE. **Staff are NOT to dress out until they meet the prerequisite criteria.**

During the Incident

- After the completion of each work rotation requiring PPE use, the staff member is to have post-entry medical monitoring done. The elements of this exam are the same as the pre-entry exam. They are to be recorded on the staff member's Medical Monitoring Incident Response record. If significant changes in the clinical data are found or subjectively offered information indicates the need for more comprehensive evaluation or medical treatment, the staff member is to be sent to the Emergency Department. The Emergency Department should be given a pre-alert ASAP about the staff member's pending arrival.
- Staff dressing out in PPE for a second work rotation are to have another pre-entry medical monitoring evaluation before donning PPE if the last exam performed was: (a) abnormal or (b) greater than 2 hours old.

After the Incident is Over

- Once the incident is declared over, the Medical Monitoring Incident Response Records for all staff are to be reviewed by the charge Emergency Department MD or Occupational Health MD to determine if any further short- or long-term clinical evaluation is necessary. If the decision is made that additional evaluation is needed, the staff member involved is to be immediately notified by the evaluating MD and arrangements made for the exam ASAP.
- The costs associated with any follow-up evaluation or treatment associated with the incident will be the responsibility of the hospital.
- Each staff member's Medical Monitoring Incident Response record is to be put into their personnel file and kept secure and retrievable for a period not less than 30 years following their retirement or resignation.

Example 2. U.S. Coast Guard National Strike Force

1. Medical Monitoring

- Medical monitoring shall be conducted on all entry, backup, and decon personnel prior to Exclusion Zone entries. Follow-up medical monitoring shall also be conducted on all entry, backup, and decon personnel at the conclusion of each work shift. For workers wearing impermeable chemical protective clothing, workers shall also be monitored when the temperature in the work area exceeds 70°F (21° C). Medical monitoring shall be conducted during the rest period following each work cycle in accordance with chapter 8 of reference 1. If the work cycle specified in Table 8-10 of Reference 1 is less than 30 minutes, the supervisor may consult the Commanding Officer for authorization to extend the work cycle up to 30 minutes.

- Recommended values from the American Heart Association are to be used as guidance for pre-entry medical monitoring:

  Blood Pressure (Max): 140 bpm Systolic/100 Diastolic*

  Pulse Rate (Max): 100 bpm

  Temperature: 98.0° F (Min), 99.2° F (Max) (or +/- 0.6° F from normal)

- When a medical value is found to be outside the accepted guidance, the supervisor should be informed immediately. Anomalous readings require medical advice prior to continued entries by an individual.

- Use appropriate forms to record field medical monitoring.

- When questions regarding medical monitoring arise, the unit Safety and Occupational Health Coordinator (SOHC) shall be contacted.

* Note: At the onset of an incident, fear and anxiety may cause employees' blood pressure to be elevated.

2. Heat Stress (adapted from NIOSH Publication No. 86-112 "Working in Hot Environments")

HEAT STROKE

Heat stroke is the most serious of health problems associated with working in hot environments. It occurs when the body's temperature regulatory system fails and sweating becomes inadequate. The body's only effective means of removing excess heat is compromised with little warning to the victim that a crisis stage has been reached.

A heat stroke victim's skin is hot, usually dry, red or spotted. Body temperature is usually 105° F or higher, and the victim is mentally confused, delirious, perhaps in convulsions, or unconscious. Unless the victim receives quick and appropriate treatment, death can occur.

Any person with signs of symptoms of heat stroke requires immediate hospitalization. However, first aid should be immediately administered. This includes removing the victim to a cool area, thoroughly soaking the clothing with water, and vigorously fanning the body to increase cooling. Further treatment, at a medical facility, should be directed to the continuation of the cooling process and the monitoring of complications which often accompany the heat stroke. Early recognition and treatment of heat stroke is the only means of preventing permanent brain damage or death.

HEAT EXHAUSTION

Heat exhaustion includes several clinical disorders having symptoms which may resemble the early symptoms of heat stroke. Heat exhaustion is caused by the loss of large amounts of fluid by sweating, sometimes with excessive loss of salt. A worker suffering from heat exhaustion still sweats but experiences extreme weakness or fatigue, giddiness, nausea, or headache. In more serious cases, the victim may vomit or lose consciousness. The skin is clammy and moist, the complexion is pale or flushed, and the body temperature is normal or only slightly elevated. In most cases, treatment involves having the victim rest in a cool place and drink plenty of liquids. Victims with mild cases of heat exhaustion usually recover spontaneously with this treatment. Those with severe cases may require extended care for several days. There are no known permanent effects.

HEAT CRAMPS

Heat cramps are painful spasms of the muscles that occur among those who sweat profusely in heat, drink large quantities of water, but do not adequately replace the body's salt loss. The drinking of large quantities of water tends to dilute the body's fluids, while the body continues to lose salt. Shortly thereafter, the low salt level in the muscles causes painful cramps. The affected muscles may be part of the arms, legs, or abdomen; but tired muscles (those used in performing the work) are usually the ones most susceptible to cramps. Cramps may occur during or after work hours and may be relieved by taking salted liquids by mouth.

FAINTING

A worker who is not accustomed to hot environments and who stands erect and immobile in the heat may faint. With enlarged blood vessels in the skin and in the lower part of the body due to the body's attempts to control internal temperature, blood may pool there rather than return to the heart to be pumped to the brain. Upon lying down, the worker should soon recover. By moving around, and thereby preventing blood from pooling, the patient can prevent further fainting.

HEAT RASH

Heat rash, also known as prickly heat, is likely to occur in hot, humid environments where heat is not easily removed from the surface of the skin by evaporation and the skin remains wet most of the time. The sweat ducts become plugged, and a skin rash soon appears. When the rash is extensive or when it is complicated by infection, prickly heat can be very uncomfortable and may reduce a worker's performance. The worker can prevent this condition by resting in a cool place part of each day and by regularly bathing and drying the skin.

TRANSIENT HEAT FATIGUE

Transient heat fatigue refers to the temporary state of discomfort and mental or psychological strain arising from prolonged heat exposure. Workers unaccustomed to the heat are particularly susceptible and can suffer, to varying degrees, a decline in task performance, coordination, alertness, and vigilance. The severity of transient heat fatigue will be lessened by a period of gradual adjustment to the hot environment (heat acclimatization).

PREPARING FOR WORK IN THE HEAT

Adjustment to heat, under normal circumstances, takes about a week, during which time the body will undergo a series of changes that will make continued exposure to heat more endurable. With each succeeding daily exposure, hazardous physiological responses will gradually decrease, while the sweat rate will increase. When the body becomes acclimated to the heat, the worker will find it possible to perform work with less strain and distress.

Gradual exposure to heat gives the body time to become accustomed to higher environmental temperatures. Heat disorders in general are more likely to occur among workers who have not been given time to adjust to working in the heat or among workers who have been away from hot environments and who have gotten accustomed to lower temperatures. Hot weather conditions of the summer are likely to affect the worker who is not acclimatized to heat. Likewise, workers who return to work after a leisurely vacation or extended illness may be affected by the heat in the work environment. Whenever such circumstances occur, the worker should be gradually reacclimatized to the hot environment.

Heat stress depends, in part, on the amount of heat the worker's body produces while a job is being performed. The amount of heat produced during hard, steady work is much higher than that produced during intermittent or light work. Therefore, one way of reducing the potential for heat stress is to make the job easier or lessen its duration by providing adequate rest. Rather than be exposed to heat for extended periods of time during the course of a job, workers should, wherever possible, be permitted to distribute the workload evenly over the day and incorporate work-rest cycles. Work-rest cycles give the body an opportunity to get rid of excess heat, slow down the production of internal body heat, and provide greater blood flow to the skin.

REST AREAS

Providing cool rest areas in hot work environments considerably reduces the stress of working in those environments. There is no conclusive information available on the ideal temperature for a rest area. Rest areas should be as close to the work area as possible, and provide shade. Individual work periods should not be lengthened in favor of prolonged rest periods. Shorter but frequent work-rest cycles are the greatest benefit to the worker.

DRINKING WATER

In the course of a day's work in the heat, a worker may produce as much as 2 to 3 gallons of sweat. Because so many heat disorders involve excessive dehydration of the body, it is essential that water intake during the workday be about equal to the amount of sweat produced. Most workers exposed to hot conditions drink less fluids than needed because of an insufficient thirst drive. A worker, therefore, should not depend on thirst to signal when and how much to drink. Instead, the worker should drink 5 to 7 ounces of fluids every 15 to 20 minutes to replenish the necessary fluids in the body. There is no optimum temperature of drinking water, but most people tend not to drink warm or very cold fluids as readily as they will cool ones. Whatever the temperature of the water, it must be palatable and readily available. Individual drinking cups should be provided—never use a common drinking cup.

Heat acclimatized workers lose much less salt in their sweat than do workers who are not adjusted to the heat. The average American diet contains sufficient salt for acclimatized workers even when sweat production is high. If for some reason, salt replacement is required, the best way to compensate for the loss is to add a little extra salt to the food. Salt tablets SHOULD NOT be used.

CAUTION—PERSONS WITH HEART PROBLEMS OR THOSE ON A "LOW SODIUM" DIET WHO WORK IN HOT ENVIRONMENTS SHOULD CONSULT A PHYSICIAN ABOUT WHAT TO DO UNDER THESE CONDITIONS.

PROTECTIVE CLOTHING

Clothing inhibits the transfer of heat between the body and the surrounding environment. Therefore, in hot jobs where the air temperature is lower than skin temperature, wearing clothing reduces the body's ability to lose heat into the air. When air temperature is higher than skin temperature, clothing helps to prevent the transfer of heat from the air to the body. The advantage of wearing additional clothes, however, may be nullified if the clothes interfere with the evaporation of sweat (such as rain slickers or chemical protective clothing).

Example 3. NIOSH Publication No. 86-112
Working in Hot Environments

HEAT STRESS CONSIDERATIONS

The Site Safety Officer or Site Safety Supervisor for the entire response should make heat stress determinations throughout the day. If it is determined that a heat stress hazard exists, an alert should be passed to all teams to implement mandatory rest periods. The Site Safety Officer/Supervisor should generally be guided by the American Conference of Governmental Industrial Hygienists (ACGIH) guidelines in determining work/rest periods. Fluids should be available at all times and encouraged during mandatory rest periods.

SAFETY CONCERNS

Certain safety problems are common to hot environments. The frequency of accidents, in general, appears to be higher in hot environments than in more moderate environmental conditions. One reason is that working in a hot environment lowers the mental alertness and physical performance of an individual. Increased body temperature and physical discomfort promote irritability, anger, and other emotional states which sometimes cause workers to overlook safety procedures or to divert attention from hazardous tasks.

HEALTH CONCERNS

Excessive exposure to a hot work environment can bring about a variety of heat-induced disorders.

Heat Stroke

SIGNS AND SYMPTOMS. Heat stroke is the most serious of health problems associated with working in hot environments. It occurs when the body's temperature regulatory system fails and sweating becomes inadequate. The body's only effective means of removing excess heat is compromised with little warning to the victim that a crisis stage has been reached.

- A heat stroke victim's skin is hot, usually dry, red or spotted.
- Body temperature is usually 105° F or higher.
- The victim is mentally confused, delirious, perhaps in convulsions, or unconscious.

MEDICAL ATTENTION. Unless the heat stroke victim receives quick and appropriate treatment, DEATH CAN OCCUR.

Any person with signs or symptoms of heat stroke requires immediate hospitalization.

SEND SOMEONE TO GET MEDICAL ASSISTANCE/EMT IMMEDIATELY!!!

While waiting for medical assistance, first aid should be immediately administered.

This includes:

- removing the victim to a cool area,
- thoroughly soaking the clothing with water, and
- vigorously fanning the body to increase cooling.

Heat Exhaustion

Heat exhaustion includes several clinical disorders having symptoms which may resemble the early symptoms of heat stroke. Heat exhaustion is caused by the loss of large amounts of fluid by sweating, sometimes with excessive loss of salt.

SIGNS AND SYMPTOMS. A worker suffering from heat exhaustion:

- still sweats, but
- experiences extreme weakness or fatigue, giddiness, nausea, or headache.

In more serious cases:

- the victim may vomit or lose consciousness,
- the skin is clammy and moist,
- the complexion is pale or flushed, and
- the body temperature is normal or only slightly elevated.

MEDICAL ATTENTION. General treatment:

- notify the site EMT,
- have the victim rest in a cool place, and
- have the victim drink plenty of liquids.

Victims with mild cases of heat exhaustion usually recover spontaneously with this treatment. Those with severe cases may require extended care for several days. There are no known permanent effects.

Heat Cramps

SIGNS AND SYMPTOMS. Heat cramps are painful spasms of the muscles that occur among those who sweat profusely in heat, drink large quantities of water, but do not adequately replace the body's salt loss.

MEDICAL ATTENTION. Cramps may occur during or after work hours and may be relieved by taking salted liquids by mouth.

Fainting

A worker who is not accustomed to hot environments and who stands erect and immobile in the heat may faint.

SIGNS AND SYMPTOMS. With enlarged blood vessels in the skin and in the lower part of the body due to the body's attempts to control internal temperature, blood may pool there rather than return to the heart to be pumped to the brain.

MEDICAL ATTENTION. Upon lying down, the worker should soon recover. By moving around, and thereby preventing blood from pooling, the patient can prevent further fainting.

Heat Rash

Heat rash, also known as prickly heat, is likely to occur in hot, humid environments where heat is not easily removed from the surface of the skin by evaporation and the skin remains wet most of the time.

SIGNS AND SYMPTOMS. The sweat ducts become plugged, and a skin rash soon appears. When the rash is extensive or when it is complicated by infection, prickly heat can be very uncomfortable and may reduce a worker's performance.

MEDICAL ATTENTION. Workers can prevent this by resting in a cool place part of each day and by regularly bathing and drying the skin.

Transient Heat Fatigue

Transient heat fatigue refers to the temporary state of discomfort and mental or psychological strain arising from prolonged heat exposure. Workers unaccustomed to the heat are particularly susceptible and can suffer, to varying degrees, a decline in task performance, coordination, alertness, and vigilance.

PREPARING FOR WORK IN THE HEAT

One of the best ways to reduce the heat stress of workers is to minimize heat in the workplace. However, heat is difficult to control while working outdoors and exposed to various weather conditions.

Humans are, to a large extent, capable of adjusting to the heat. This adjustment to heat, under normal circumstances, usually takes about 5 to 7 days, during which time the body will undergo a series of changes that will make continued exposure to heat more endurable.

Workers who return to work after vacation or extended illness may be affected by the heat in the work environment. Whenever such circumstances occur, the worker should be gradually reacclimatized to the hot environment.

MECHANIZATION

Heat stress depends, in part, on the amount of heat the worker's body produces while a job is being performed. The amount of heat produced during hard, steady work is much higher than that produced during intermittent or light work. Therefore, one way of reducing the potential for heat stress is to make the job easier or lessen its duration by providing adequate rest time. Mechanization of work procedures can often make it possible to isolate workers from the heat source and increase overall productivity by decreasing the time needed for rest.

WORK/REST PERIODS

Rather than be exposed to heat for extended periods of time during the course of a job, workers should, wherever possible, be permitted to distribute the workload evenly over the day and incorporate work-rest cycles or regular (and enforced) breaks. Work-rest cycles give the body an opportunity to get rid of excess heat, slow down the production of internal body heat, and provide greater blood flow to the skin.

Providing cool rest areas in hot work environments considerably reduces the stress of working in those environments. Rest areas should be as close to the work area as possible, and provide shade. Shorter but frequent work-rest cycles are the greatest benefit to the worker.

DRINKING FLUIDS

In the course of a day's work in the heat, a worker may produce as much as 2 to 3 gallons of sweat. Because so many heat disorders involve excessive dehydration of the body, it is essential that water intake during the workday be about equal to the amount of sweat produced.

Most workers exposed to hot conditions drink less fluids than needed because of an insufficient thirst drive. A worker, therefore, should not depend on thirst to signal when and how much to drink.

Five to 7 ounces of fluids should be consumed every 15 to 20 minutes to replenish the necessary fluids in the body.

There is no optimum temperature of drinking water, but most people tend not to drink warm or very cold fluids as readily as they will cool ones.

Heat acclimatized workers lose much less salt in their sweat than do workers who are not adjusted to the heat. The average American diet contains sufficient salt for acclimatized workers even when sweat production is high. If for some reason, salt replacement is required, the best way to compensate for the loss is to add a little extra salt to the food.

Salt tablets SHOULD NOT be used.

CAUTION—PERSONS WITH HEART PROBLEMS OR THOSE ON A "LOW SODIUM" DIET WHO WORK IN HOT ENVIRONMENTS SHOULD CONSULT A PHYSICIAN ABOUT WHAT TO DO UNDER THESE CONDITIONS.

PROTECTIVE CLOTHING AND HEAT STRESS

Clothing inhibits the transfer of heat between the body and the surrounding environment. Therefore, in hot jobs where the air temperature is lower than skin temperature, wearing clothing reduces the body's ability to lose heat into the air. When air temperature is higher than skin temperature, clothing helps to prevent the transfer of heat from the air to the body. The advantage of wearing additional clothes, however, may be nullified if the chemical protective clothes interfere with the evaporation of sweat.

Example 1. Vital Signs and PPE Checklist
(Central Arkansas Veterans Healthcare System)

NAME

DATE

>> INSPECT condition of ALL PPE prior to use <<

*Medical Exclusion

Employee ID#:

	PRE	POST
BLOOD PRESSURE:		
*Diastolic > 105		
HEART RATE:		
* > [70% (220 – Age)]		
*Any irregular rate or rhythm		
RESPIRATION:		
* > 24 / min		
TEMPERATURE:		
* > 99.5 deg F oral		
WEIGHT:		
SKIN:		
*Open sore, large rash or sunburn		
HYDRATION:		
MENTAL STATUS:		
Alert; oriented to time & place; clear speech; normal gait		

MEDICAL HISTORY:
*Any meds last 72 hours
*Alcohol past 24 hours
*New meds Rx / diagnosis last 2 weeks
*Symptoms fever, NV, diarrhea,
  cough in past 72 hours
*Pregnant
*Prior heat stress or exhaustion

PAPR–COMBINATION CARTRIDGES..... ☐

PAPR FLOW CHECKED.......................... ☐

REMOVED SHOES, JEWELRY, ETC....... ☐

INNER NITRILE GLOVES..................... ☐

INNER SUIT... ☐

GLOVES & NECK TAPED.................... ☐

OUTER SUIT....................................... ☐

BUTYL HOOD...................................... ☐
        INNER SHROUD TUCKED INSIDE

GLOVES & NECK TAPED.................... ☐

OUTER GLOVES.................................. ☐

BOOTS... ☐

SUIT TAPED OVER BOOTS .... ☐

NOTES:

CHECKED BY:

TIME IN SUIT:

CHECKED BY:

TIME OUT:

Source:
Central Arkansas Veterans Healthcare System

OSHA
Occupational Safety and
Health Administration

Example 2. Vital Signs Monitoring Checklist
(U.S. Coast Guard National Strike Force)

ON-SITE MEDICAL MONITORING (ENTRY TEAM)

NAME:

CASE: CASE NO.:

DATE: EXPOSURE RISK: HIGH / MED / LOW

PROTECTIVE EQUIPMENT:

SUBSTANCE(S) INVOLVED:

CONCENTRATION/LENGTH OF EXPOSURE

MEDICAL TESTING:

COMMENTS:

PRE-ENTRY MEDICAL MONITORING:

WEIGHT: TEMPERATURE: METHOD:

PULSE: BP: SYSTOLIC   /DIASTOLIC   METHOD:

MONITORING CONDUCTED BY:

POST-ENTRY MEDICAL MONITORING:

WEIGHT: TEMPERATURE: METHOD:

PULSE: BP: SYSTOLIC   /DIASTOLIC   METHOD:

MONITORING CONDUCTED BY:

SUPERVISOR (RO/RS) VERIFICATION:

NAME:

COMMENTS:

Source:
U.S. Coast Guard National Strike Force

Patient Decontamination Procedure
(Northern Virginia Emergency Response Coalition)

AMBULATORY PATIENTS

1. Direct patient to Decon Sector.

2. Children should be kept with their parents if at all possible; if no parent or older sibling is available then a Decon Team member should provide needed assistance to a child.

3. Patient should be given Personal Decon set as soon as it is available and be given rapid instructions on its use – PLAY THE TAPE recorded set of instructions, if available.
   • The kit stays with you as you proceed through the process.
   • Open up the bag – it has three parts.
   • Take out the plastic bags now.

4. Patient should quickly remove all clothing, putting valuables into the clear plastic bag and clothing into the large bag, then put both bags into the 3rd bag and cinch tight w/ tag number in pack. Patient should put numbered tag around their neck and wear it through decon and treatment.

5. The clothing bag should be set aside in a secure area.

6. If staff is available, patient's name and number should be recorded on the Patient Decon Record.

7. Patient should continue forward into the Decon Sector with remaining part of Personal Decon Kit.

8. Patient should quickly rinse themselves from head to toe with water using either the hand held sprayer, garden hose, or showerhead.

9. Patient should next wash with soap and wash cloth or brush from the kit in a systematic fashion, cleaning open wounds first and then in a head-to-toe

Source:
Northern Virginia Emergency Response Coalition. Available at: http://www.hazmatforhealthcare.org/download/doc/misc/Patient_Decontamination_Procedure-complete.doc (Accessed September 2, 2003).

fashion for 5 minutes when the agent is non-persistent and 8 minutes when a persistent or unknown agent is involved. Discourage the patient from rubbing too vigorously while washing. Eye irritation may require the use of a topical anesthetic first before irrigating.

10. The Decon Team should closely observe each victim to ensure they are thorough in washing themselves. Particular attention should be made to ensure they wash the axilla, creases, folds, and hair. Help should be offered as necessary.

11. Once the washing is completed, each patient should thoroughly rinse themselves (this should require about a minute to complete).

12. Decon soap, wash cloths, brushes, and sponges should be put into a nearby trash can and NOT carried into the Cold Zone.

13. After the rinse/wash/rinse cycle is complete the patient should next proceed to the towel off area and complete drying off and leave the towel in the trash can.

14. Following drying off, the patient should put on the patient gown and proceed to the Triage Officer for rapid assessment and assignment to a Treatment Sector.

15. Additional treatment will be limited only to those interventions deemed life saving by the Decon Officer. Antidote administration should be done via the intramuscular (IM) route after cleaning the affected area first.

16. Decon Team members should be alert to the possibility that an ambulatory patient may clinically deteriorate and require immediate removal to the Non-Ambulatory Sector via backboard, stretcher, or wheelchair.

NON-AMBULATORY PATIENTS

1. Patient should be brought to the Decon Sector and tended to by a minimum of 4 decon personnel.

2. Each patient should be put onto a backboard or EMS stretcher w/ the pad removed.

OSHA
Occupational Safety and
Health Administration

3. All patient clothing should be removed and valuables put into the clear plastic bag and clothing into the large bag, then put both bags into the 3rd bag and cinch tight w/ tag number in pack. Clothing should be cut away where necessary.

4. Attention should be paid to minimizing the aerosolization spread of particulate matter by folding clothing inside out as removal is being done and dabbing the skin with sticky tape and/or vacuuming.

5. Patient should have their clothing bag tag around their neck and wear it through decon and treatment.

6. The clothing bag should be set aside in a secure area. If staff is available, the patient's name and number should be recorded on the Patient Decon Record.

7. While resting the backboard on saw horses or other device or with the patient on an EMS stretcher, the patient should quickly be rinsed from head to toe with water using either the hand held sprayer, garden hose, or showerhead; protection from aspiration of the rinse water should be ensured.

8. Next the patient should be washed with soap and either a brush or wash cloth in a systematic fashion, cleaning airway first followed by open wounds then in a head to toe fashion for 5 minutes when the agent is non-persistent and 8 minutes when a persistent or unknown agent is involved. Avoid rubbing too vigorously.

9. The patient should be rolled on their side for washing of the posterior head, neck, back, buttocks and lower extremities by 2–4 personnel; attention to a possible neck injury should be given.

10. Careful attention should be given to washing the voids and creases such as the ears, eyes, axilla, and groin.

11. Topical eye anesthetic may be required for effective eye irrigation to be done.

12. The patient should then be rinsed in a head to toe fashion that minimizes contamination spread for about one minute. Overspray or holding the rinsing device too close so as to irritate the skin should be avoided.

13. Decon Team members should be alert to the probability that the non-ambulatory patient may require ABC's support (airway positioning, suctioning, O_2 administration, spinal stabilization, etc.) and administration of life saving antidote administration by IM injection. If IV therapy is needed the extremity site for the IV should be deconned quickly before the IV is started. If IV therapy is needed the patient should be pulled out of line in the Decon Corridor but remain in the Decon Sector.

14. The patient should be dried off, put into a hospital gown, and transferred to a clean backboard (or clean off and dry the board they are on if additional boards are not available). Patients on an EMS stretcher should be transferred to a clean backboard.

15. Decon soap, brushes and sponges should be put into a trash can and not carried into the Cold Zone. O_2 material should remain in the Decon Sector.

16. The patient should be taken to the Triage Officer for rapid assessment and assignment to area in the Treatment Sector.

PATIENTS WITH SPECIAL NEEDS
Glasses/Contact Lenses
1. Patients with glasses should keep them if they cannot see without them. They must be washed and rinsed thoroughly during the decon process before being worn. Otherwise, the glasses should be placed in the valuables portion of the clothing bag.

2. Contact lenses should be removed and placed in the valuables portion of the clothing bag.

Canes/Walkers
1. Patients who use walking assist devices may retain them, but the device must be washed with soap and water during the decon process before being allowed into the Treatment Sector.

2. Patients who are unsteady standing and/or walking should be given a walker upon entry into the Decon Corridor. The walker should be used to assist with ambulation until they get to the end of the line when it should be retrieved, deconned, and returned to the front of the Decon Corridor for the next patient who needs it.

Percutaneous Lines/Saline Locks

1. Unless contaminated, percutaneous lines and saline locks should be covered with Tegoderm or Saran wrap before the area is decontaminated.

2. Contaminated percutaneous lines or saline locks should be removed before being decontaminated. After the area is cleaned, a dressing should be applied until in the Treatment Sector where antibiotic ointment and a new bandage should be applied.

Hearing Aids

1. Hearing aids CANNOT be immersed or otherwise be soaked with water. Thus, they should either be removed and placed in the valuables portion of the patient's clothing bag or if they must be used by the patient because there is no hearing without them, they should be carefully wiped off with a slightly saline moistened 4x4 gauze, dried off, put into a clear plastic bag, and handed to the patient. The cleaned hearing aid is NOT to be worn until the patient has completed the decon process (including washing the ears) and is in the Treatment Sector.

Dentures

1. Unless the oral cavity is contaminated, dentures should remain in place and no decontamination is necessary.

2. If the oral cavity is contaminated, then the dentures should be removed, placed in a clear plastic bag with the patient's name or clothing identification number placed on it. The dentures should later be decontaminated in accordance with instructions received from the Poison Center and/or a dentist. The patient's mouth should be decontaminated with mouthwash or saline that is gargled and safely spit out into a bio-hazard bag. Note that, depending on the contaminant, it may not be possible to decontaminate plastic items, such as dentures.

Law Enforcement Officers with Weapons

1. In most cases, law enforcement personnel who have been injured on the scene will have had their gun(s) removed before arrival and given to a fellow officer. However, if that is not the case, the weapon should be left in the holster and the gun belt removed by a Decon Team member and placed in a clear plastic bag labeled with the patient's name and/or clothing number. The bag should then be passed to the Treatment Sector where it should be given to a fellow officer or hospital Security Officer for safe keeping until it can be given to a representative of the injured officers department. **THE GUN SHOULD BE LEFT IN THE HOLSTER IF AT ALL POSSIBLE.** If the gun must be removed, it should be handled by a Decon Team member familiar with firearms, rendered safe, placed in a clear plastic bag marked with the patient's name and/or clothing identification number, and given to a fellow officer or hospital Security Officer in the Treatment Sector.

2. Decon Team personnel should be aware that oftentimes an officer may have a backup weapon usually found in a holster near the ankle, in their pocket, in a ballistic vest, or near an armpit. The holster with the weapon in place should be removed and secured as described above.

3. An officer's gun belt may also contain items that could prove dangerous if allowed to get in the wrong hands. Thus, the belt should be collected and separately bagged ASAP and passed to a fellow officer or hospital Security Officer in the Treatment Sector. **DECONNING OF AN OFFICER'S WEAPON AND/OR GUN BELT WILL BE THE RESPONSIBILITY OF THE POLICE DEPARTMENT.**

4. If the officer is wearing a ballistic vest it must be removed prior to undergoing decon. The vest is usually easily removed by loosening the Velcro® straps and then pulling the vest apart and off the patient. It should then be placed in a large plastic bag identified with the patient's name and/or clothing number on it and passed to a fellow officer or Hospital Security Officer in the Treatment Sector.

Prepared by:
Northern Virginia Emergency Response Coalition

PPE Donning Sequence

(NOTE: The following sequence outlines the *order* in which one hospital's employees find it efficient to put on their specific first receiver PPE. The list is not intended to provide detailed step-by-step instructions for putting on the PPE.)

1. Test PAPR flow rate to be sure it meets rate specified by the manufacturer.

2. Remove jewelry & clothing.

3. Put on inner nitrile gloves.

4. In COLD WEATHER: Put on inner suit. Tape gloves at wrist & zipper at neck.

5. In WARM WEATHER: Put on scrubs.

6. Put on outer chemical protective suit to waist. Put on boots & outer chemical protective gloves.

7. Connect PAPR to hood with hose; turn airflow on. Put on butyl hood (position the inside shroud between suits). Pull chemical protective suit up and on.

8. Ensure zipper is covered & secured, put tape on top.

9. Belt PAPR to waist.

10. Put outer butyl hood shroud over suit.

11. Stretch arms, pull suit sleeves OVER gloves, tape in place.

12. Pull suit cuff over boot top, tape in place.

13. Place a piece of tape on the hood exterior and label with the employee's name & time that employee is entering Hospital Decontamination Zone.

PPE Decontamination and Doffing Sequence

(NOTE: The following sequence outlines the *order* in which one hospital's employees find it effective to decontaminate themselves and their PPE as one procedure, to minimize the chance of contaminating their skin while removing their first receiver PPE. The list is not intended to provide detailed step-by-step instructions.)

1. Wash hands thoroughly.

2. Still wearing PPE, wash self, starting at the top of the head and working down to the bottom of the boots. Have a partner wash your back.

3. Untape boots and gloves, but do not remove them.

4. Unlock PAPR and place it on chair/gurney/floor, etc.

5. Remove the outer suit—roll the suit away from you, inside out (with help from a partner). Remove outer gloves along with the outer suit.

6. Remove PAPR hood, place in waste.

7. Step out of boots and suit into final rinse area (keep inner gloves and clothing on). Wash and rinse thoroughly (with partner's help).

8. In COLD WEATHER: Remove (inner) suit, place in waste.

9. Remove nitrile gloves: first pinch one glove and roll it down partially, then place thumb in other glove & remove both gloves simultaneously.

10. Wash again, removing inner clothing, then step out of decontamination shower and into towels/blankets.

Source:
Adapted from Central Arkansas Veterans Healthcare System.

Technical Decontamination Process
for Hospital Personnel

Personnel should remove protective clothing in the following sequence.

1. Remove tape (if used), securing gloves and boots to suit.

2. Remove outer gloves, turning them inside out as they are removed.

3. Remove suit, turning it inside out and folding downward (first loosen and secure PAPR belt). Avoid shaking.

4. Remove boot/shoe cover from one foot and step over the clean line. Remove other boot/shoe cover and put that foot over the clean line.

5. Remove respirator. The last person removing his/her respirator may first wash all other respirator hoods or facepieces with soapy water and thoroughly wipe PAPR fan housing, then clean his/her own equipment before removing his/her suit and gloves. Place the masks in plastic bag and hand the bag over the clean line for placement in second bag held by another staff member. Send bag for decontamination. Discard items that cannot be effectively cleaned (e.g., it may not be possible to completely remove persistent contaminants from PAPR belts).

6. Remove inner gloves and discard them in a drum inside the dirty area.

7. Secure the dirty area until the level of contamination is established and the area is properly cleaned.

8. Personnel should then move to a shower area, remove undergarments and place them in a plastic bag. Double-bag all clothing and label bags appropriately.

9. Personnel should shower and redress in normal working attire and then report for medical surveillance.

Source:
Adapted from *Managing Hazardous Materials Incidents. Hospital Emergency Departments: A Planning Guide for the Management of Contaminated Patients.* Volume II. U.S. Department of Health and Human Services. Public Health Service. Agency for Toxic Substances and Disease Registry (Revised 2000). www.atsdr.cdc.gov

OSHA
Occupational Safety and
Health Administration

Note: The *Emergency Management and Disaster Preparedness Plan—Chemically contaminated patient care protocol* included in this appendix was developed by the INOVA Health System (Virginia) for use in INOVA facilities. The INOVA Health System uses powered air-purifying respirators (PAPRs). However, in cases where information is adequate to determine that an air-purifying respirator (APR) would provide adequate protection against the hazard, APRs might be used in place of PAPRs. At INOVA facilities, a specific, designated individual (the *Charge MD*) is responsible for determining the appropriate PPE for the decontamination team and for making appropriate adjustments as the situation evolves.

This example plan represents a portion of the emergency management plan used by one healthcare organization. Based on their individual circumstances, other organizations will have different procedures, terminology, and division of responsibilities.

 INOVA HEALTH SYSTEM

Policy #:   Disaster Plan, 2002 Rev, <u>Envir of Care Safety Manual</u>

<u>Emergency Management Plan</u>

INOVA HEALTH SYSTEM
Emergency Management & Disaster Preparedness Plan

Subject: ANNEX C- Chemically Contaminated
Patient Care Protocol

Written: August 5, 2002   Revision:

Emergency Management and Disaster Preparedness Task Force

PURPOSE: To establish a policy for providing care to victims of hazardous materials and/or chemical terrorism incidents while ensuring the safety of the emergency department (ED) personnel and hospital environment.

BACKGROUND: The potential for hazardous materials exposure requires specific procedures for the protection of the patient, staff, and the environment. It differs from the other emergency situations because of that added risk of contamination to staff and facility. Worker safety and training are key factors in the management of these medical emergencies. Often these patients may arrive at the hospital unannounced. Patients being transported by EMS may not have been fully decontaminated prior to their arrival to the hospital.

TOXICOLOGICAL
PRINCIPLES: Exposure to hazardous materials may produce a wide range of adverse health effects. The likelihood of an adverse health effect occurring, and the severity of the effects, are dependent upon:

- The toxicity of the agent or pathogen
- Route of exposure
- The nature and extent of exposure to that substance

Toxic chemical effects may be localized at the site of exposure, or may result in systemic symptomatology after absorption into the blood stream.

The three main routes of exposure are:
- **Inhalation** resulting in the introduction of toxic chemicals, radioisotopes, or pathogens via the respiratory tract. Most of the compounds that are inhaled are gases or vapors of volatile liquids. However, solids and liquids can be inhaled as dusts or aerosols. Inhalation of chemical agents generally result in a rapid absorption into the bloodstream because of the large surface and vascularity of the lungs. The signs and symptoms of pathologic exposure will usually occur 1–10 days after exposure.
- **Skin contact** or absorption via mucous membranes is usually not as rapid as inhalation. Exposure can be through the mucus membranes (including conjunctiva) and open wounds.
- **Ingestion** is a less common route of exposure. It can be the result of unintentional hand to mouth contamination or swallowing of saliva with trapped airborne particles. Or it may also be intentional, such as an oral ingestion for a suicide attempt.

In addition to the route of exposure, the amount of compound absorbed by the body depends upon the:
- Duration of exposure
- Concentration of contaminant
- Time of exposure
- Environmental factors

Response to toxic chemicals, radiological agents and pathogens may differ among individuals because of the physiological variability present in the population.
- Age
- Preexisting medical conditions
- Prior exposure
- Medications
- Concurrent injury
- Pregnancy

NOTIFICATION:

Unannounced Arrival refers to a patient(s) that presents to the ED Triage Nurse or other healthcare provider. Once the healthcare provider determines a hazardous materials incident has occurred and contamination may be present he/she should:
- Direct the patient outside the ED lobby entrance and proceed to the entryway of the decon room. Confine the patient in this location and remain with them.
- Notify the charge nurse.
- Notify security at Triage to secure the area.
- Any persons the victim came in contact with, including the initial healthcare provider contact, should also be directed to the decon room until the extent of contact and the need for care can be determined.
- If there are multiple patients affected, prepare to implement the mass decontamination procedure utilizing identified areas outside of the hospital facility but contiguous to the ED.

Announced Arrival is a patient already entered into the EMS system that arrives by ambulance. The major advantage created by pre-hospital notification is the provision of preparatory time and available clinical data and incident information from the field

as well as initial intervention by EMS personnel. The arriving patient should be kept with the pre-hospital EMS personnel outside of the ED until the "decontamination team" is prepared to assume patient care.

Consultation with the referring agency as to the decontamination, if any, performed at the incident scene must occur prior to admitting these patients directly into the ED. This should depend upon the nature of the agent, degree of decontamination provided in the field, and suspicion of potential contamination upon visual inspection of the patient. If in doubt, have the patient go through decontamination at the hospital.

EMERGENCY DEPARTMENT RESPONSIBILITIES

Communication Nurse
- Determine caller's ID and telephone number.
  - Type and nature of incident
  - Number of victims
  - Signs and symptoms being experienced by victim
  - Nature of injuries
  - Prior medical history of victim – meds and allergies
  - Name of chemical involved and what information is readily available on product container if present
  - Name of facility involved and/or type of contaminants found at facility
  - Extent of victim decontamination in field
  - Other medical interventions completed
  - Estimated time of arrival (ETA)
- Notify charge nurse.
- Notify EMS Public Safety Communications Center (PSCC) of incident and request redirection of other ambulance traffic to ED lobby entrance.
- If incident involves multiple patients, request that ED be placed on "reroute" status.

Charge Nurse
- Consult with charge MD and assess the present patient capacity and acuity. If incident involves multiple patients, implement **"Disaster Plan – Annex C."**
- Expedite movement of "admitted" patients to assigned beds.
- Notify the ED Patient Care Director and Administrative Director as to the status of incoming contaminated patients. Consider the need for additional staff and resources and initiate response, if warranted.
- Initially assign 2 nurses and 2 techs to the decontamination team.
- Notify ED registration, triage nurse, and security.
- Notify respiratory therapy and determine the number of adult/pediatric ventilators.
- Determine number of available adult/pediatric beds.

Administrative Director
- Notify security officers to redirect ED traffic and ambulances.
- Notify physical plant staff.
- Notify environmental services.
- Notify Personal Health for follow-up on staff involved.
- Notify Media Relations to be available for purpose of public information if needed.
- Notify Administrator-on-call that **"Disaster Plan – Annex C"** is being implemented.

Charge MD
- Confer with ED Charge Nurse regarding the immediate need to implement the **"Disaster Plan – Annex C"** and assess the disposition status of existing patients in the ED.
- Notify ED Chairman.
- Notify Poison Control–obtaining available product info to decontaminate and care for patient(s), when available.
- Notify critical care pharmacist with product info for anticipated antidote. Obtain inventory of available antidotes.
- Determine appropriate level of Personal Protective Equipment (PPE) for Decon Team.
- Assign MD and/or PA to Decon Team.
- Direct 1–2 personnel to set up decon area and 1–2 persons to assist decon team with dress out procedures.

Security
- Secure entrances and exits to the ED.
- Assist with traffic and crowd control around the ED.
- Will be responsible for maintaining "chain of custody" of personal belongings of patients undergoing decontamination. These items will NOT be individually catalogued, but rather placed in red biohazard plastic bags that will be tagged, numbered, and recorded.

DECONTAMINATION PURPOSE:

To remove or neutralize harmful materials that have gathered on personnel and/or equipment and to prevent secondary contamination to healthcare workers and the facility. Decontamination is a systematic process that is determined by the nature and degree of contamination. Effective decontamination consists of making the patient as clean as possible, meaning that the contamination has been reduced to a level that is no longer a threat to the patient or healthcare provider.

DECON SETUP:

In a "traditional" HAZMAT incident involving known exposure to chemical agents involving less than 3 patients simultaneously, consideration can be given to using the existing Emergency Department Decontamination Room, if available.

Decon room preparation tech shall be assigned to:
- Remove all non-essential and nondisposable equipment and items from established Hazmat/Decon wash room.
- Activate drain switch to contain runoff, if available.
- Obtain decon cart with necessary stocked items.
- Obtain crash cart and place contiguous to Decon wash room.
- Place D or E size O_2 tank with regulator.
- Place clean stretcher in Hazmat/Decon wash room with additional O_2 tank, BVM, and non-rebreather mask.
- Place stretcher outside of decon room on plastic ground cloth to receive non-ambulatory patient from ambulance.
- Place bucket for soiled items used in wash room for technical decon.
- Place lined trash baskets in decon area for Biowaste.
- Place Personal Decon Kits (PDK) in decon area.

Mass Decontamination Setup

In the event that the chemical exposure incident involves more than 3 people requiring decontamination simultaneously, or incident information suggests the arrival of large numbers of patients requiring decontamination as a result of a mass exposure, preparation for mass decontamination should commence.

The following materials have been identified as basic prerequisites for Mass Decontamination set up and preparation:

- A hose bib splitter for each bib within 100 feet (within range) of the proposed decontamination area.
- Two 100-foot hoses for each hose bib within range of the proposed decontamination area.
- Four (2 sets) sawhorses to hold litter bound patients within the decontamination area and set of C-clamps.
- Two backpack sprayers per facility.
- Two baby pools per facility.
- Four buckets for each hose bib within range of the proposed decontamination area.
- Four scrub brushes for each hose bib within range of the decontamination area.
- Duct tape, flashlights, permanent markers, soap, large trash cans, red biohazard bags, and towels.
- One blood pressure cuff, stethoscope, and set of trauma scissors per litter decontamination station.
- Towels and redress kits.
- Two Geiger counters per facility (Reference **"Disaster Plan – Annex R"**).
- Two Bull horns per facility.
- Polaroid camera with film or digital camera for later use in identification of moribund patients.
- A locked, centrally located storage mechanism (cart, closet, etc.) for storage of the aforementioned items.

Included in this Annex is a schematic diagram for use in establishing a Mass Decontamination procedure that details the process flow of patients. This should be adapted to each individual healthcare facility.

LEVEL C PERSONAL PROTECTIVE EQUIPMENT

Decon team preparation

1. Obtain appropriate personal protective equipment (PPE) as recommended by ED charge physician.

2. A minimum of 4 persons should don PPE.

3. Decon team personnel should undergo pre-entry medical monitoring as soon as possible. Only personnel meeting inclusion criteria, and having met the required training standards will be allowed to dress in PPE.

4. The Inova Health System has elected to use LEVEL C respiratory protection and chemical protective clothing as the highest level of protection available. LEVEL C respiratory protection is comprised of:

- **Powered Air Purifying Respirator (PAPR)**: This provides air that is drawn through organic/HEPA filter cartridges affixed to a battery powered unit worn by the decon team personnel on a belt around their waist. It is worn as a hood placed over the head, with the inner sleeve tucked into the chemical protective clothing suit.
- **Air Purifying Respirator (APR)**: This provides air that is filtered through organic/HEPA filter cartridges dependent on the negative inspiration created by the work of breathing. This is worn as a full-face mask with the cartridges affixed to the mask.

Caution: These respiratory protective equipment contain LATEX products and are not to be worn by LATEX-allergic individuals.

LEVEL C chemical protective clothing is contained in the Tri-con PPE packs that include:
- 2 layers of gloves
- chemical resistant suit (check for appropriate sizing)
- chemical resistant boots

Note: Some Tri–Con PPE packs will also contain an APR mask. Consult with the ED physician in charge with regards to selection of APR or PAPR. Persons needing to use glasses, or those with beards or full moustaches, are NOT to use a face mask device.

A Decon team member should double check to assure all personnel have donned their PPE properly. Special attention should be paid to proper seal of mask/face and proper occlusion at wrists and ankles. Particular attention must be made to ensure all "pull tabs" are removed from respiratory cartridge filters prior to use.

Immediately evaluate the available information and confirm/re-confirm (as more information becomes available) that your key *operational* planning assumptions for Level C PPE are valid:
- Incident location (including area of significant downwind contamination) does not include your facility.
- Agent characteristics: Known or suspected agent doesn't require higher level of PPE (example: high-grade plutonium or other very rare agents).
- Event characteristics: Your facility is not being "overrun" by casualties.

Adjust the planned operations as indicated by the evolving circumstances. Possible adjustments include:
- Upgrading plan: more personnel protected, shorter rotation periods for PPE personnel, longer soap & wash cycles for victims, obtaining assistance from other hospitals or from emergency response resources.
- Evacuating or closing the facility to "shelter in place" if the hospital is in the zone of contamination.
- "Lock-down" of facility if agent, agent concentration, or the number of patients exceeds the safe operation of the plan or compromises the hospital integrity.
- Any need to isolate the decontamination wastewater (notify authorities to remove it per prior arrangement). Otherwise, notify "downstream" water authorities that decontamination wastewater is entering the sewer system.
- Downgrade the plan (lesser protective clothing and/or respiratory protection if agent is identified as non-threatening). This should be a high priority if possible, since safely downgrading the level of PPE will enhance the efficiency of the decontamination process.

Donning Procedures: Staff medical monitoring to be completed by assigned

Registered Nurse (RN) or MD (use designated medical monitoring form included in this Annex). Use a room with privacy and plenty of sitting space to facilitate donning of PPE.

1. It is preferable that a scrub suit be worn in lieu of regular street clothes. Clothing should be suitable for preserving comfortable body temperature.

2. Remove all jewelry and leather material and place in plastic bag with your name on it—place in secure location for Security to maintain. Persons needing to wear glasses or with beards or mustaches are NOT to use a face mask device.

3. Persons with long hair should apply a hairnet or place up in a braid.

4. Hydrate with 8–16 ounces of fluid.

5. If time allows have blood pressure (BP), pulse, respiration rate, and temperature taken and recorded on Medical Surveillance form.

6. Obtain appropriate sized PPE ensemble pack or individual pieces, APR/PAPR, battery, and appropriate cartridges (2–3 depending on APR/PAPR being used).

7. Layout PPE pieces and confirm they are right size and in working order.

8. Apply appropriate type of cartridges (most incidents will require HEPA/organic vapor cartridge set) and remove all pull-tabs. DO NOT OVERTIGHTEN the cartridges on the mask.

9. Put on latex or plastic inner glove—consider placing light circular band around top of glove to lessen chance of premature removal during doffing.

10. While sitting, remove shoes and place on foot covers (foot protection should not present tear risk to the suit nor be heelless).

11. Pull on chemical/biological protective suit to waist.

12. Place outer booties/boots on over the foot portion of the suit.

13. Using duct tape, seal top of booties to protective coverall (use a flap of tape at the end and place facing front to ease removal).

14. For chemical incident, place one set of nitrile gloves and one set of butyl rubber gloves on hands. For biological incident, use double plastic/latex gloves or plastic/latex and nitrile gloves.

15. Seal seam of protective suit and gloves with duct tape (use a flap of tape at the end and on the front of the wrist area to ease removal of tape).

16. Zip up protective suit to neck and close zipper securing and covering zipper seal.

17. If using PAPR, put on vest. Cinch up vest to snug fitting around with motor unit riding above the buttocks. Secure battery to the belt (side of the dominant hand is

suggested) and plug in the PAPR. The air hose should come over the shoulder not under the arm.

18. Position APR/PAPR facepiece to ensure full visibility and comfortable fit. Tighten all bands in pairs by pulling them backwards and not up. Confirm tight seal by covering cartridge opening with hand and taking deep breaths—face shield should pull tight against face. If faulty seal is found, then retighten all bands and repeat seal test. If tight seal cannot be obtained, then seek second provider assistance or use hooded device.

19. Pull suit hood up and over the head maximizing the coverage of the head, neck, and ears and covering the APR/PAPR seal edge around the face–ensure the suit is pulled up and fully under the chin and zipper is closed and covered. There should be NO EXPOSED SKIN.

20. Turn PAPR on, also making sure that all cartridge tabs are removed to allow airflow.

21. Have someone place a 3 in. piece of Velcro$^{®}$ or tape across shoulders with staff member's last name and function (e.g., Jones RN) written with magic marker.

22. Have second person perform safety check before proceeding to assigned work area.

23. Note time personnel left the dress out area.

Ambulatory Patient Decontamination

- Children should be kept with their parents if at all possible; if no parent or older sibling is available then a Decon Team member should provide needed assistance to a child.
- Patient should be given Personal Decon kit as soon as it is available and be given rapid instructions on its use.

The ambulatory patient may be directed by the decon nurse and tech to self-decon in the Emergency Department Decontamination Room thereby sparing additional staff from involvement (though the full decon team should remain dressed and ready in an adjacent room if intervention is needed). If the situation involves multiple patients requiring simultaneous decontamination, this process will occur using the Mass Decontamination set up.

1. If dry contaminant, remove first by using tape or dust off clothing or skin before wetting.

2. Have patient remove all valuables and place in the small plastic bag.

3. Clothing is removed and placed in the larger plastic bag. Place both bags into the red biohazard plastic bag. Place identifying tag with unique patient number on bag and seal off top. Place outside on ramp area for future disposition by Safety and Security.
4. Patient will do head-to-toe gross decontamination wash using mild soap and

water. Have patient place ID band around wrist. This ID band will have the same identifying number that has been placed on the red biohazard plastic bag holding the patient's personal effects.

5. Special attention should be paid in the washing process to hair and all body crevices. Wash time cycle should be 5 (five) minutes per person under a single stream of water.

6. Water temperature should be tepid.

7. Washing should be gentle to avoid abrading skin.

8. Open wounds should be washed first with sterile water and covered with occlusive dressing prior to remainder of body decontamination.

9. Upon completion of wash cycle, patient should step away from the immediate wash area, towel dry, and put on a supplied Tyvek® gown from the Patient Redress Kit.

10. All ED towels and wash cloths used by patients in the showering process should be placed in a marked contaminated container for later clean up and decontamination.

11. Patient may then enter the ED, where the receiving RN can obtain vital signs, complete secondary triage, complete decon paperwork, and transport to an assigned bed in ED.

12. Decon team personnel should be decontaminated prior to entering the ED as described in Personnel (Technical) Decon section.

13. Soap should be changed out every five patients or whenever needed.

Non-Ambulatory Patients
In a mass exposure to chemical agents, non-ambulatory patients will most likely arrive after the initial arrival of ambulatory patients exposed in the same geographic location. Because of the trimodal distribution of injuries, non-ambulatory patients are likely to be more significantly exposed to the contaminating agent. Those who are most severely affected will be in the expectant category at the incident scene, and those who are least affected or only "potentially exposed" will arrive as ambulatory patients.

The non-ambulatory patient decontamination should be performed simultaneously with patient stabilization. Basic life support (ABC's) will be maintained, but definitive intervention should be delayed until the patient is decontaminated to a degree that ensures staff safety and that invasive procedures will not increase the patient's risk of systemic toxic absorption. If large numbers of non-ambulatory patients are delivered for decontamination and treatment simultaneously, the ED Charge Physician will be required to make urgent triage decisions.

1. Patient should be received on a backboard and stretcher by EMS staff. If incident involves a single non-ambulatory patient, utilization of the Emergency Department

Decon Room may be considered. If multiple patients are expected, set up of the non-ambulatory mass decontamination corridor should commence.

- Placement of saw horses with available C-clamps in order to secure backboards to the sawhorses.
- Availability of water source for adequate decontamination, including use of back-pack sprayers.

2. The Decon team for non-ambulatory patients must include a minimum of four (4) providers, two of whom will be responsible for turning the patient on the backboard and one who will be responsible for maintaining cervical spine precautions.

3. If the patient has not had a primary gross decon in the field (defined as the removal of clothing and first wash), visible particulate matter should be removed by gently brushing or dusting, and clothing should be cut and rolled away from the center of body, in order to contain the contaminants on the clothing.

4. Follow procedure for removal and bagging of personal valuables.

5. Follow procedure for head-to-toe decontamination wash cycle.

6. Irrigate open wounds with irrigation syringe and copious amounts of saline and cover with occlusive dressings. Any existing dressing must be removed and placed in bio-hazard trash container.

7. Eye irrigation may be done with Morgans lens and NS and/or IV tubing alone, if gross contaminants on the face are suspected. Otherwise, perform manual irrigation with copious fluids.

8. Gentle ear and nasal irrigation with frequent suctioning from portable suction may be done if such contamination is suspected.

9. C-collars as well as backboards must be washed or changed if they are still required for patient immobilization.

10. Patient should be transferred to a clean stretcher for entry into the ED.

Personnel (Technical) Decon
Prior to leaving the decon room the decontamination team must undergo decontamination.

1. All equipment used by the decon staff must be placed in appropriate receptacles or in bins designated for equipment which can be cleaned and reused. Refer to clean-up and recovery protocol for direction on rehabilitation of used equipment.

2. Decon staff will undergo a technical decontamination wash from head-to-toe involving the outer garments, gloves, and boots.

3. After the wash is complete, personnel should remove protective clothing in the following sequence:
- Remove outer gloves, turning them inside out as they are removed and place in bio-hazard trash container.

OSHA
Occupational Safety and
Health Administration

- Remove tape from wrist and boot tops.
- Remove boots.
- Remove suit, turning inside out and avoid shaking.
- Remove APR mask or PAPR hood. The last member removing his/her respiratory protective equipment may take responsibility for washing all masks in soapy water. Refer to clean-up and recovery protocol.
- Remove inner glove and discard into bio-hazard trash container.
- Isolate all potentially contaminated materials until level of contamination is established and arrangements for cleaning and handling of trash and equipment can be determined.
- Post-exposure medical monitoring should be initiated and new data recorded on the primary form.
- Personnel should then remove scrub wear and shower and dress in replacement scrubs.

Emergency Decon
- Staff member distress is recognized.
- Staff member PPE immediately decontaminated with soap and water.
- PPE removed quickly in head to toe fashion in cold zone area. Medical care rendered as warranted.

KEY RESOURCES/POINTS OF CONTACT

Notifications of appropriate authorities:
Law Enforcement-
   Local Police Department
   Federal Bureau of Investigation/DC [202-324-3000]
Fire/Rescue Department
Local Health Department
State Health Department
   Emergency Epidemiology After Hours [1-866-820-9611]
National Capital Region Poison Control Center [202-625-3333]
Agency for Toxic Substances and Disease Registry (ATSDR) [1-404-498-0120]
National Response Center [1-800-424-8802]

IN-HOSPITAL HAZMAT INCIDENT

- Contain victims in area of incident until contamination is confirmed.
- Administrative Director to be notified by area supervisor of incident site and specifics.
- Hospital operator, notified by area supervisor, shall page ED charge nurse with HAZMAT location.
- Hospital operator shall page Safety and Security to restrict access to the site.
- ED charge nurse and ED charge physician assign HAZMAT team for response to site ONLY if patients are identified to be immediately in danger of exposure.
- If Emergency Department HAZMAT team required to respond within facility have the communication nurse call PSCC to request ED "reroute" status and request Fire Department HAZMAT response per facility protocol.
- The HAZMAT team should then dress in appropriate level of PPE for the given response. If unknown contaminant, dress in highest level of protection available.
- The HAZMAT team responds to site bringing portable decontamination equipment

for decontamination at a safe area closest to the site of incident.
  - Single patient – non-ambulatory bring 2 stretchers, one with containment cover and hose and container for runoff collection.
  - Ambulatory – bring kiddy pools (2) and backpack sprayers or large irrigation bottles for decon wash.
- Decon shall be completed at site (as in previously described manner) until patient is clean enough for transport to ED for more definitive decon.
- Transport to ED shall be on the clean stretcher with a clean transport team.
- ED HAZMAT team to complete personal decon at the incident site prior to return to ED.

MEDICAL MONITORING

The need to perform ongoing medical monitoring of those healthcare personnel participating in the decontamination procedure is **MANDATORY**. This entails a systematic evaluation of all participants, focusing particular attention to the risk of suffering adverse reactions from heat, stress or hazardous materials exposure. This is performed for the purpose of prevention or early recognition of such symptoms, and in compliance with federal regulations.

Medical monitoring is performed prior to donning PPE in order to:
- Ascertain baseline vital signs.
- Identify staff who will be disqualified from donning PPE and participating in the decontamination process due to pre-existing medical conditions.
- Identify staff who may be at a higher risk for potential adverse effects while working in this environment.

Pre-entry physicals are required on all individuals in protective clothing and performing hazardous material operations. This is to be completed within one hour prior to entry, when possible.

PRE-ENTRANCE EXAM COMPONENTS

- Vital Signs
  - Blood pressure, pulse, respiration rate, temperature
  - Weight (estimated)

- Skin evaluation for presence of:
  - Rashes
  - Lesions
  - Open wounds

- Mental Status evaluation, including assessment of psychological stressors.

- Medical History
  - Chronic illnesses
  - Recent illnesses
  - Medications, including OTC taken within the past 72 hours
  - Current symptoms of fever, nausea, diarrhea, vomiting, coughing, wheezing, or recent alcohol consumption.

- Exclusion Criteria

OSHA
Occupational Safety and
Health Administration

- Blood pressure:	diastolic over 95
- Pulse:	greater than 70% maximum heart rate (220 - age) x 0.7
	irregular rhythm not previously documented
- Respiratory rate:	greater than 24 per minute
- Temperature:	less than 97 or greater than 99.5
- Weight or Size:	inability to fit in available suit without causing undue strain on seams
- Skin evaluation:	open sores, large areas of rash, or significant sunburn
- Mental status:	any alteration
- Recent medical history:	nausea, vomiting, diarrhea within the past 72 hours, recent heat related injury, new prescriptions started within the past 72 hours.

- Pregnancy

ALL STAFF MUST BE CLEARED FOR PARTICIPATION BY THE ED CHARGE PHYSICIAN PRIOR TO PARTICIPATION.

- ENTRY Medical Monitoring
  - Performed before donning PPE.
  - Based on buddy evaluation by team member.
  - Observe for changes in gait, speech or behavior.
  - Any complaints of chest pain, dizziness, SOB, weakness, headache, nausea or vomiting should be reported.
  - Reporting of symptoms requires immediate personnel decon and removal from the decon site.
  - Personnel data should be recorded on HAZMAT Medical Monitor form (see attached).

- POST-ENTRY Medical Monitoring
  - Vital signs repeated every 10 minutes until return to less than 85% of maximum pulse rate.
  - Oral rehydration started immediately upon completion of personal decon.
  - IV hydration and more aggressive medical evaluation shall be initiated for victims displaying medical illness and/or unstable vital signs.

- The completed Hazmat Medical Monitoring form shall be forwarded to Employee Health for review and decision, if further evaluation is needed. The assessment form is to become part of the individual's occupational health file.

EQUIPMENT/SUPPLY ACQUISITION

If needed equipment and supplies are not available in the ED, the ED charge physician should be notified immediately. This information should then be immediately forwarded to the **DISASTER SUPPORT CENTER**, which can help procure needed materials. If all on-site resources have been exhausted, the Inova Health System **DISASTER COMMAND CENTER** will be contacted by the hospital Disaster Support Center in order to identify location of needed supplies and additional logistical support.

CLEAN-UP AND RECOVERY

Upon completion of the decontamination process, consideration must be given immediately to the following issues:

• Personal belongings and valuables of patients

These items will be in tagged, sealed red biohazard bags kept outside of the health-care facility under the direct supervision of the hospital Safety and Security staff, or local law enforcement personnel. These items may not be returned until they are deemed safe for handling and their evidentiary content has been evaluated.

• Bio-hazard trash can contents

These trash cans will contain soaps, sponges, scrub brushes, towels, and other items used by patients during the decontamination process. These bags must be sealed and segregated for later removal by contract waste haulers.

• Towel discard bins

These bins will hold the towels discarded by patients who have completed the decontamination process just prior to their entry into the healthcare facility. These bags must be segregated for possible laundering or later removal by contract waste haulers.

• Wastewater effluent

In the event that mass decontamination efforts are required, the importance of life safety concerns supercedes the potential environmental impact of contaminated effluent. Every attempt should be made to direct this effluent into the sanitary sewer, with immediate notification of the proper municipal agencies. In those cases in which only limited numbers of patients are involved, every attempt should be made to contain this effluent using "baby pools" or similar methods. Such collected water must then be properly disposed of under the direction and supervision of the appropriate municipal agencies and contract waste haulers.

Any area outside of the healthcare facility that was used in the mass decontamination process and was inside of the WARM or HOT ZONES must be cordoned off until such time as it is verified by hazardous materials experts that no risk of contamination exists.

OSHA Assistance

OSHA can provide extensive help through a variety of programs, including technical assistance about effective safety and health programs, state plans, workplace consultations, voluntary protection programs, strategic partnerships, training and education, and more. An overall commitment to workplace safety and health can add value to your business, to your workplace and to your life.

Safety and Health Program Management Guidelines

Effective management of worker safety and health protection is a decisive factor in reducing the extent and severity of work-related injuries and illnesses and their related costs. In fact, an effective safety and health program forms the basis of good worker protection and can save time and money (about $4 for every dollar spent) and increase productivity and reduce worker injuries, illnesses and related workers' compensation costs.

To assist employers and employees in developing effective safety and health programs, OSHA published recommended *Safety and Health Program Management Guidelines* (54 *Federal Register* (16): 3904-3916, January 26, 1989). These voluntary guidelines apply to all places of employment covered by OSHA.

The guidelines identify four general elements critical to the development of a successful safety and health management program:

- Management leadership and employee involvement.
- Work analysis.
- Hazard prevention and control.
- Safety and health training.

The guidelines recommend specific actions, under each of these general elements, to achieve an effective safety and health program. The *Federal Register* notice is available online at www.osha.gov

State Programs

The Occupational Safety and Health Act of 1970 (*OSH Act*) encourages states to develop and operate their own job safety and health plans. OSHA approves and monitors these plans. Twenty-four states, Puerto Rico and the Virgin Islands currently operate approved state plans: 23 cover both private and public (state and local government) employment; 3 states, Connecticut, New Jersey and New York, cover the public sector

only. States and territories with their own OSHA-approved occupational safety and health plans must adopt standards identical to, or at least as effective as, the Federal standards.

Consultation Services

Consultation assistance is available on request to employers who want help in establishing and maintaining a safe and healthful workplace. Largely funded by OSHA, the service is provided at no cost to the employer. Primarily developed for smaller employers with more hazardous operations, the consultation service is delivered by state governments employing professional safety and health consultants. Comprehensive assistance includes an appraisal of all mechanical systems, work practices and occupational safety and health hazards of the workplace and all aspects of the employer's present job safety and health program. In addition, the service offers assistance to employers in developing and implementing an effective safety and health program. No penalties are proposed or citations issued for hazards identified by the consultant. OSHA provides consultation assistance to the employer with the assurance that his or her name and firm and any information about the workplace will not be routinely reported to OSHA enforcement staff.

Under the consultation program, certain exemplary employers may request participation in OSHA's Safety and Health Achievement Recognition Program (SHARP). Eligibility for participation in SHARP includes receiving a comprehensive consultation visit, demonstrating exemplary achievements in workplace safety and health by abating all identified hazards and developing an excellent safety and health program.

Employers accepted into SHARP may receive an exemption from programmed inspections (not complaint or accident investigation inspections) for a period of one year. For more information concerning consultation assistance, see the OSHA website at www.osha.gov

Voluntary Protection Programs (VPP)

Voluntary Protection Programs and on-site consultation services, when coupled with an effective enforcement program, expand worker protection to help meet the goals of the *OSH Act*. The three levels of VPP are Star, Merit, and Demonstration designed to recognize outstanding achievements by companies that have successfully incorporated comprehensive safety and health programs into their total management system. The VPPs motivate others to achieve excellent safety and health results in the same outstanding way as they establish a cooperative relationship between employers, employees and OSHA.

For additional information on VPP and how to apply, contact the OSHA regional offices listed at the end of this publication.

Strategic Partnership Program

OSHA's Strategic Partnership Program, the newest member of OSHA's cooperative programs, helps encourage, assist and recognize the efforts of partners to eliminate serious workplace hazards and achieve a high level of worker safety and health. Whereas OSHA's Consultation Program and VPP entail one-on-one relationships between OSHA and individual worksites, most strategic partnerships seek to have a broader impact by building cooperative relationships with groups of employers and employees. These partnerships are voluntary, cooperative relationships between OSHA, employers, employee representatives and others (e.g., trade unions, trade and professional associations, universities and other government agencies).

For more information on this and other cooperative programs, contact your nearest OSHA office, or visit OSHA's website at www.osha.gov

Alliance Programs

The Alliances Program enables organizations committed to workplace safety and health to collaborate with OSHA to prevent injuries and illnesses in the workplace. OSHA and the Alliance participants work together to reach out to, educate and lead the nation's employers and their employees in improving and advancing workplace safety and health.

Groups that can form an Alliance with OSHA include employers, labor unions, trade or professional groups, educational institutions and government agencies. In some cases, organizations may be building on existing relationships with OSHA that were developed through other cooperative programs.

There are few formal program requirements for Alliances and the agreements do not include an enforcement component. However, OSHA and the participating organizations must define, implement and meet a set of short- and long-term goals that fall into three categories: training and education; outreach and communication; and promoting the national dialogue on workplace safety and health.

OSHA Training and Education

OSHA area offices offer a variety of information services, such as compliance assistance, technical advice, publications, audiovisual aids and speakers for special engagements. OSHA's Training Institute in Arlington Heights, IL, provides basic and advanced courses in safety and health for Federal and state compliance officers, state consultants, Federal agency personnel, and private sector employers, employees and their representatives.

The OSHA Training Institute also has established OSHA Training Institute Education Centers to address the increased demand for its courses from the private sector and from other Federal agencies. These centers are nonprofit colleges, universities and other organizations that have been selected after a competition for participation in the program.

OSHA also provides funds to nonprofit organizations, through grants, to conduct workplace training and education in subjects where OSHA believes there is a lack of workplace training. Grants are awarded annually. Grant recipients are expected to contribute 20 percent of the total grant cost.

For more information on grants, training and education, contact the OSHA Training Institute, Office of Training and Education, 2020 South Arlington Heights Road, Arlington Heights, IL 60005, (847) 297-4810 or see "Outreach" on OSHA's website at www.osha.gov. For further information on any OSHA program, contact your nearest OSHA area or regional office listed at the end of this publication.

Information Available Electronically

OSHA has a variety of materials and tools available on its website at www.osha.gov. These include *e-Tools* such as *Expert Advisors, Electronic Compliance Assistance Tools (e-cats), Technical Links*; regulations, directives and publications; videos and other information for employers and employees. OSHA's software programs and compliance assistance tools walk you through challenging safety and health issues and common problems to find the best solutions for your workplace.

A wide variety of OSHA materials, including standards, interpretations, directives, and more, can be purchased on CD-ROM from the U.S. Government Printing Office, Superintendent of Documents, phone toll-free (866) 512-1800.

OSHA
Occupational Safety and
Health Administration

OSHA Publications

OSHA has an extensive publications program. For a listing of free or sales items, visit OSHA's website at www.osha.gov or contact the OSHA Publications Office, U.S. Department of Labor, 200 Constitution Avenue, NW, N-3101, Washington, DC 20210. Telephone (202) 693-1888 or fax to (202) 693-2498.

Contacting OSHA

To report an emergency, file a complaint or seek OSHA advice, assistance or products, call (800) 321-OSHA or contact your nearest OSHA regional or area office listed below. The teletypewriter (TTY) number is (877) 889-5627.

You can also file a complaint online and obtain more information on OSHA Federal and state programs by visiting OSHA's website at www.osha.gov

OSHA Regional Offices

Region I
(CT,* ME, MA, NH, RI, VT*)
JFK Federal Building, Room E340
Boston, MA 02203
(617) 565-9860

Region II
(NJ,* NY,* PR,* VI*)
201 Varick Street, Room 670
New York, NY 10014
(212) 337-2378

Region III
(DE, DC, MD,* PA, VA,* WV)
The Curtis Center
170 S. Independence Mall West
Suite 740 West
Philadelphia, PA 19106-3309
(215) 861-4900

Region IV
(AL, FL, GA, KY,* MS, NC,* SC,* TN*)
61 Forsyth Street, SW
Atlanta, GA 30303
(404) 562-2300

Region V
(IL, IN,* MI,* MN,* OH, WI)
230 South Dearborn Street
Room 3244
Chicago, IL 60604
(312) 353-2220

Region VI
(AR, LA, NM,* OK, TX)
525 Griffin Street, Room 602
Dallas, TX 75202
(214) 767-4731 or 4736 x224

Region VII
(IA,* KS, MO, NE)
City Center Square
1100 Main Street, Suite 800
Kansas City, MO 64105
(816) 426-5861

Region VIII
(CO, MT, ND, SD, UT,* WY*)
1999 Broadway, Suite 1690
PO Box 46550
Denver, CO 80202-5716
(720) 264-6550

Region IX
(American Samoa, AZ,* CA,* HI,* NV,* Northern Mariana Islands)
71 Stevenson Street, Room 420
San Francisco, CA 94105
(415) 975-4310

Region X
(AK,* ID, OR,* WA*)
1111 Third Avenue, Suite 715
Seattle, WA 98101-3212
(206) 553-5930

* These states and territories operate their own OSHA-approved job safety and health programs (Connecticut, New Jersey and New York plans cover public employees only). States with approved programs must have a standard that is identical to, or at least as effective as, the Federal standard.

Note: To get contact information for OSHA Area Offices, OSHA-approved State Plans and OSHA Consultation Projects, please visit us online at www.osha.gov or call us at 1-800-321-OSHA.